GIST

THE ESSENCE OF RAISING LIFE-READY KIDS

Michael W. Anderson, LP
Timothy D. Johanson, MD

GIST
The Essence of Raising Life-Ready Kids

Originally published by GISTWorks, LLC, Minneapolis, MN in a slightly
different form.

ISBN 13: 978-1-59298-635-4
Library of Congress Catalog Number: 2016902582
Printed in the United States of America
Third Printing: 2017
20 19 18 17   6 5 4 3

BEAVER'S
POND
PRESS

Beaver's Pond Press, Inc.
7108 Ohms Lane Edina, MN 55439–2129
(952) 829-8818
www.BeaversPondPress.com

To order, visit www.ItascaBooks.com or call (800) 901-3480

Printed in the United States of America

TABLE OF CONTENTS

Part II - Core Development

To children everywhere who simply want
to be raised in homes where grace, love,
firmness, and consistency are abundant.

To parents who strive to raise their children
to be ready for life.

Acknowledgments

This project started out in dialogue form ten years ago as an idea spawned from meetings with a dozen other couples struggling with the parenting endeavor. The manuscript got its beginnings on an island in Canada, and became a reality in a cottage on the Northern Ireland coast, overlooking the Irish Sea.

It has been an endeavor that has taken us from our respective practices to places of intense reflection, and from the comfort and confidence of our own experiences as dads to humbling places of personal realization. It's the closest thing we can imagine to childbirth, knowing full well most women who have birthed a child would laugh at that claim.

With that said, we need to give some thanks and offer our deep gratitude to several very important people in our lives who have put up with us individually and as a writing team. Our wives, Carolyn Anderson (Mike) and Susan Johanson (Tim), have been a constant support over many years. They believe in what we do in our professional lives and what we have attempted to do with them for our own children and foster children. Both our wives are extremely wise women, phenomenal moms, and wonderful companions with whom to travel the parenting journey. Our children, Kellan, Reid, and Brieg Anderson and Annika, Emily, and Luke Johanson, have been the greatest source of joy for us, as well as challenge. What part we have played in their amazing journeys we will never know.

The thousands of our clients, patients, and their parents have made our lives meaningful. It has been a privilege and honor to come alongside them to help them in some small way. Our respective staffs, co-workers, partners, nurses, and lab personnel all have made that process easier for us and we are thankful for them all.

Although not a complete list by any means, the following individuals and entities deserve special mention: Tim Proue, Doug Berg, Bob Dykstra, Michele Tennesen, Inger Logelin, and Metropolitan Pediatric Specialists.

Michael W. Anderson, LP
Timothy D. Johanson, MD

INTRODUCTION

This book just wouldn't go away.

Both of us, in our own ways, tried to push it off for a decade or more. For the longest time we couldn't quite see how to write a book about "how to" parent when the "how to" advice nearly always started with, "That depends ..." In both our respective offices, parents sat in the waiting room and hoped they would learn some way to "treat" the presenting problem, whatever that happened to be.

We were repeatedly struck that the presenting problem was usually not the real problem. Bad grades, stress symptoms, frequent fussing, defiance, depression, self-destructive behavior, and conflict often brought families in for help. But the real problem was that the families were stuck, tired, angry, and confused about where their problem came from. They didn't know what to do and they wanted that behavior, fear, and pain to stop *now*.

We found ourselves helping parents think differently about a situation and were amazed at how quickly the problem improved or disappeared simply by seeing it in a new and accurate light. *We came to believe that the best hope in addressing parenting issues is by thinking differently about parenting issues.*

That is what motivated us to capture these thoughts and stories in a book. Thinking better won't solve every parenting challenge, as parenting is a difficult and formidable task. But better thinking is our best chance of making parenting successful, enjoyable, and hopeful.

We certainly don't intend to imply that healthy parenting is rare or non-existent. However, there can be no denying that too many parents are tired and lost these days. For parents who are drowning, this book could be a lifeboat. For the parents who are doing well, this book will be a pleasant and validating read as they learn more about the wisdom of their own approach.

Long before we met, we were both troubled by how stressed-out kids seemed to be growing up, and we both chose careers that gave us the privilege to watch and learn. This book came out of our experience spending, collectively, over fifty years listening to kids in our offices, then listening to their parents, then listening to kids, and then the parents. When we first met, we would spend hours discussing why we sounded like we were contradicting ourselves, when we knew we weren't. There isn't one right way to fall in love, to chase a dream, to have a career, or to grow spiritually—and there isn't one right way to parent.

A parent recently asked us at a workshop, "What should I do if my seventh-grade son leaves his homework on the kitchen counter when he leaves for school in the morning?"

"That depends on your son," we answered. "Tell us about your son. Overall, is he a fairly responsible seventh grader?"

"Oh yes, he's extremely responsible for his age."

"Then just jump in the car and run his book up to the school. And by the way, stick two dollars in his math book for a sports drink. You don't need to teach a responsible son to be responsible. He already knows that—he just forgot his homework. You have other things to teach him that are more relevant."

If the son had been perpetually irresponsible, we would have recommended a different approach. One-size-fits-all parenting would most likely recommend teaching him a lesson he didn't need to learn while adding needless strain to the whole process.

How to parent a situation will depend on what areas your child is doing well with and in which areas he or she is falling behind. We feel a good parenting book will show how and why one child should be parented differently than another child—or the neighbor's kids. Here's the thing: We don't know your children and where they come from. Are they biological or adopted? Are you a single parent or two-parent family? Do your children have reading disabilities or social limitations? Are they depressed or angry? All these will affect your choices on what to do.

Good parenting needs to be learned and practiced, since it doesn't come naturally for most people. In fact, much of parenting is counterintuitive. The natural thing to do is often the wrong thing to do so we need to learn new skills and practice them until they start to feel natural. For example, too many reprimands—even those with best intentions—might actually hurt a situation without our awareness. Even the desire to be a "great parent" could hurt our ability to parent our child effectively and efficiently. It may sound like a good thing, but parents who are overly concerned with how well they are doing may lose perspective and become too emotionally involved in a situation to think clearly. Therefore new skills are more effective than more effort.

We want parenting to be easier and more effective because wasted energy is a big problem for parents today. Many hours and much emotional energy are spent in parenting strategies where nothing positive is produced. We hope this book will be practical and helpful. Perhaps it will even be a breath of fresh common sense to an endeavor that has become far too complicated and laborious.

As professionals working with children and teenagers, we have both recognized that kids today need to be raised in a way that reduces stress, shame, and resentment. Too many kids struggle with discouragement, so we have taken an extensive look at where this comes from. Perhaps the most pervasive struggle for older kids is their awareness that they are not ready for life. We have seldom come across any child older than ten who doesn't have some fear that adulthood will arrive before he or she is ready.

We have rarely met a child who didn't innately value and respect any adult who exhibits the combined character qualities of wisdom, kindness, strength, honesty, firmness, and humility. While kids act and talk like they just want their own way, upon closer scrutiny, they really want adults in their lives that they can lean against as they do the hard work of growing up, without it damaging the adult's feelings or their connection together.

We've chosen the title GIST as it means the bottom line, the truth, or the inner workings of something. We say, "The gist of it" when we want someone to know the way something really works. The thesis of this entire book is about preparing your kids for life, and doing that in an effective way. As we discuss what qualities a *life-ready* child would have, it seemed that it would be helpful to devote part of the book to a brief description of the nature of life, as we see it. Therefore, the first part of the book is about love, learning, living, and joy. You may have a different opinion about these foundational characteristics of life, but at least you will know where we are coming from as we reflect on these crucial topics. We need to be life-ready adults if we are going to raise life-ready kids. We encourage you to read this first section as a way to gain valuable insight for parenting in a way that focuses on all of us being life-ready.

The second section of the book is about learning solid

parenting thought processes and implementing proven strategies.

The third section takes a deeper look at the unintended consequences of ineffective parenting.

With all the stories, insights, and advice—we still know that the real power for change is learning how to think differently about parenting. We share this book as a labor of love and with excitement.

PART I

FOUNDATIONAL PRINCIPLES OF LIFE

CHAPTER ONE:
LOVE MUST EVOLVE

A child is born. Strong emotions fill us as the miracle of birth happens before our eyes. Impassioned, we reach down to touch tiny fingers and smell the unique newborn fragrance. We listen with wonder to cries, grunts, and cute little infant squeaks. This child seemingly comes out of nowhere, yet contains our DNA. She holds our inheritance within her and a world of possibilities. We are captured and fall completely in love with this tiny, vulnerable child.

Along with this love, we face an endeavor of greater magnitude, potential, and pitfalls than any we've previously known. Instinctively jolted, at least temporarily, out of self-centeredness, we step into a new level of existence. With an acute sense of the importance of the task, we realize that we have entered into *legacy* for the first time in our lives. This precious child before us is the enduring part of us that we will pass down.

When we break down the elements of this love, we are aware that this child:

- Came from me
- Needs my protection
- Is my legacy
- Has immense potential
- Is a miracle
- Is totally accepted
- Is completely vulnerable and precious

The pure love we experience in that first week of life is so uncomplicated. Not easy, but certainly uncomplicated. Many parents find that first week to be perfection—a perfect child embraced in perfect love. Eventually, this love will need to evolve into something different. In every relationship and aspect of life, love must evolve to survive.

Bringing this child home must evolve into sending that child into the world. Potential must evolve into limitation. Hope must evolve into disappointment. Perfection must evolve into reality and failure.

Because love always emerges as something other than what we hoped for and something different from how it started, it follows that our love as parents must evolve. It might even need to evolve from a "would-never-hurt" love into a "need-to-hurt" love. This little miracle may evolve into a bad dream.

When does the simple love of infancy need to start changing?

IT STARTS WITH A WILL

The journey for parents to a new love is launched when a child exhibits a will. The caring and protecting mode changes into managing differences between the will of the child and the will of the parent. Bedtime is no longer driven by a primal need for sleep—now it is driven by a child's personal desire to stay up. We start on the road to adulthood with the onset of joys and disappointments, give and take, negotiation and compromise.

Both joys and disappointments are initiated when a child starts having opinions. This exertion of demands or will is traditionally followed by wants, followed by opposing opinions, followed by conflict, leading to a relationship that is completely different than the one that began at the birthing center.

A new environment emerges from will and personal opinion. This environment includes things like authority, discipline, disappointment, relationship, and achievement. While this is not an exhaustive list, it captures a lot of the challenges facing parents. In its simplest terms, the essence of loving our children is about moving our vulnerable and beautiful child from infancy to adulthood. An understanding of authority, discipline, disappointment, relationship, and achievement will all be needed for the child to reach maturity.

Any person without a significant understanding of authority, discipline, disappointment, relationship, and achievement has not developed and is not ready for adulthood.

This is why a lot of parents reach out to get help. We hear, "My child has a problem with authority" or "My child has a problem with discipline" or "My child has a problem with relationships." Perhaps the most common is, "My child has a problem with disappointment."

Too many kids become adults with one or more of these areas under-developed or not developed at all. It is not surprising these children are under-prepared. Their parents' love did not evolve over time and the child did not learn the necessary lessons. This isn't to say the parents lacked love, only that it did not evolve.

Authority and hierarchy require a child to lay aside his will. This is a foundational truth for families and any society. Everyone has to answer to someone. Everyone must comply with laws and authority that may differ from what they want or think is fair at that moment. Without a respect for this truth, one can't be adult. To correctly love our child we must teach him or her that this is the nature of life. It's not love if we're not preparing them for this reality. This is far more loving than giving presents, trophies, and encouragement.

Another aspect of this evolution involves oppositional bonding - practicing a love that stays constant or grows, despite differing opinions. In an unhealthy family, conflict or opposition can negatively affect relationships. Kids in these families can grow up to believe that harmony is an essential part of bonding. However, healthy families allow for oppositional positions; in these families, family members can disagree without having that conflict diminish the relationship. If this ability isn't developed, conflict can feel like abandonment.

Know Where You're Headed

We won't be afraid or disillusioned by this journey if we understand where the journey is to take us. It starts with a child who is adored and protected, but it must give way over twenty years to a child who is free and equipped. That is a long journey and our destination.

How does this evolution happen? First of all, the steps that lead to maturing transitions must be done intentionally and skillfully. Except for the few truly "natural" parents who do this instinctively, most parents need to be deliberate about leading their child to a place of self-governance and being equipped for life. In our era and particularly in our western culture, many parents have become sidetracked with performance and other urgencies, while the process of ensuring that their child becomes an equipped, independent, and responsible adult suffers due to lack of focus.

> **It starts with a child who is adored and protected, but it must give way over twenty years to a child who is free and equipped.**

What if this process doesn't happen? The consequence will be a twenty-year-old with the maturity level of a fourteen-year-old. There's nothing wrong with a fourteen-year-old maturity level. It just looks awkward in someone who's twenty-something. If you wonder whether this is an exaggeration, just look around and see how many twenty-year-olds are living without direction, accountability, independence, and a sense of responsibility. Much of this can be traced back to a child who was deeply loved, but with a love that didn't evolve.

AGE-APPROPRIATE DEVELOPMENT

Knowing when and how to transition to a different kind of love is a talent that parents need to develop. It is as problematic for a two-year-old to be given freedom and responsibility as it is for a twenty year-old to be only adored and protected. In many families we can see both of these errors of focus. Some start too early in their zeal to be good parents, pushing their child from his vocabulary to his accomplishments. This type of rushing is all too common and occasionally even reaches the news.

Several years ago a seven-year-old girl crashed a small

plane in the western U.S. as she attempted to become the youngest person to fly across the entire country. She needed more protection and less self-sufficiency for this mission. In our opinion, her parents' love was not age-appropriate.

It is a wonderful thing for a child to develop in normal, healthy, and age-appropriate ways. Here are a few examples of expected tasks for a typical three-year-old:

- Learning the language that allows a child to express ideas and thoughts related to his or her environment,

- Rational counting (counts from three to five objects in a group to determine how many objects are in the group),

- Classifying objects into categories, (size, shape, color, etc.), ordering objects and identifying shapes such as squares, circles, triangles, and rectangles,

- Recognizing characteristics of different seasons and weather, and

- Beginning to observe, explore, and describe a wide variety of live animals and where they live.

You get the idea. These are not just mundane things for a three-year-old to learn, these are wonderful and amazing things for a three-year-old to learn.

There is a corresponding list of wonderful and amazing things for an eighteen-year-old to learn. Expected skills for an eighteen-year-old should include:

- Has the ability to listen to and evaluate the viewpoints of others,

- Delays gratification. Is able to put off what he or she wants to do now because there are more important things to do or because there is a better time to do it,

- Accepts the fact that he can't always win, and learns from mistakes instead of being demoralized about the outcome,

- Can differentiate between rational decision-making and emotional impulse,

- Capable of separating true love from transitory infatuation, and

- Takes ownership and responsibility for personal actions.

Those are just some of the developmental qualities a seventeen- or eighteen-year-old should be exhibiting.

Customizing Your Love

Without knowing you or your child, we can't tell you the specifics of how this transition has to take place. But, it must take place. We can't tell you how much to protect or push your eighth-grade child. Some need to be held in and some need to be pushed out. Endeavoring to know this is what an evolving love is about.

When you pay close attention to your child, it is not that difficult to know what he or she needs to focus on next. A book—even ours—may not help with this process. Instead, let your child show you what's next. Spend a little time looking at what life is like and the stage your child is at and a couple of issues will come to the forefront.

The world is perfectly fine with people of varying personality types and gift sets. There is room for children who are shy or quiet, or are the life of the party. Musical kids, athletic kids, funny kids, and serious kids are all wired differently. However, all kids need traits such as resilience and the ability to face fear, take responsibility, work hard, be kind, and handle disappointment. These life skills are universally needed. The lack of development of these skills becomes obvious. Be wise as you discern this. Love your child always and immensely—but know that he, and your love, must evolve.

Sadly, not all children are born into a situation where they are loved, accepted, and wanted. Some children enter the world with no one who truly wants to love them, welcome, and adore them. For whatever reason—teenage pregnancy, financial constraints, or addiction—neither parent can fully welcome this child. Those children face unique challenges as they learn to assimilate into a world unwilling to celebrate their birth. Their wounds will be deep and require work and courage to heal. We can only hope that they eventually find families and communities able to love them.

The GIST of It

- It's very important for parents to recall the joy and pleasure they experienced at the birth or adoption of each of their children. Remember those precious times, full of hope and anticipation. When times get tough, it's easy to forget all the good—and great—times and focus on the negatives.

- If you love your child the same way for four years, your

love is not evolving. Watch your child closely in daily life and you will figure out where and how your love needs to evolve.

- How we love our kids needs to change along the way. We cannot nurture them, compliment them, protect them, or adore them into becoming mature, life-ready young adults. It just won't happen that way. Our job is to train our children, prepare them, and in them leave a legacy. Training them for adulthood means freeing and equipping them. This is our primary role.

Chapter Two:
Learning and Anti-Learning

Have you ever had a dog that sneaks up on an off-limits couch to sleep? He knows the word "no" and that he shouldn't be on it. But, the couch is comfortable, and if he doesn't get in too much trouble, he'll likely continue to sneak up there. There's no real cost to disobeying the rule. If this dog is playfully scolded and petted for doing so, he'll continue to sleep on the couch. The dog needs a bad outcome in order to stop making a bad decision. And the outcome must be costly in the dog's world. Saying, "Bad dog" may or may not constitute a cost to the dog; that depends on the dog.

Adults, kids, pets, livestock, and show animals all learn best when one simple environment exists: when they get a good outcome from a good or desired decision and when they have a costly outcome from a bad or undesired decision. This is at the core of most learning. Perhaps no other principle is as essential to understand in parenting.

Like our pets, we are always learning. This may be a troubling truth, troubling because so much of what we learn isn't true or helpful. Some of what we learn is well founded. But, some things will need to be unlearned sometime in the future. There's a high cost to learning what is not true and has no real redeeming value. Any past learning that we later need to unlearn takes us further from the truth. It is what we will call "anti-learning."

Here's how we best learn.

TRUE LIFE LESSONS OR FALSE LESSONS

True life lessons are valuable and necessary. False lessons are highly overrated. Don't confuse the two. False lessons are setbacks, a waste of time, misleading, and unproductive. Contrary to what is often promoted by our culture, there is nothing to be gained by learning something that is false. True life lessons are often painful and laborious but they are also good in that they are essential for our growth.

We learn from our mistakes. Most of us will vigilantly defend this truism. But, it is high time we separate mistakes from false truths. We learn from mistakes, but we learn nothing from false beliefs. The price for believing false truths is far too high to smugly accept it as a plank on the platform of learning life's lessons.

What good did it do for fourteenth-century Western Europe to believe for a decade that the Black Plague was the result of sin? Did anything beneficial come from that untruth? Spiritual growth didn't occur because people of faith were confused by what they thought God was doing. Besides the devastation of the plague, communities inflicted ruthless acts on suffering individuals because they presumed it to be a judgment, instead of a disease epidemic. Their wrong guess about its source was not growth producing in any way.

This is a truth throughout human and personal history. The time we spend believing that something false is true can't be reclaimed. People use limited or false data to come to errant conclusions today, too. Sometimes we are taught wrong information that we believe to be true. Often false truths come from looking at an immediate outcome without looking at the longer-range outcome of that decision.

> It is 1:00 a.m. in a city on a dark winter night. Two teenage boys see a car idling in front of a house. The owner of the car had stopped briefly to drop off or pick up something in the neighborhood and left the car running to stay warm. In two seconds, the boys make their decision and jump into the car. They drive straight to a garage that they heard will pay cash for late model SUVs, chop them up, and sell them for parts.

Over the next couple of days these boys are going to either learn that stealing a car pays off or they are going to learn that it is too costly to do again. Life is going to support one conclusion or the other. Either this quick decision pays off or it doesn't.

Over the course of their lifetimes, if they live long enough, the boys would invariably learn that stealing cars is a bad idea. Most car thieves and drug dealers and shoplifters eventually do learn this lesson, though it may take years. But, if these boys conclude that stealing cars pays off, they have learned an untruth. Eventually, they will have to discard what they learned if they are ever going to become mature—or even survive.

Stealing cars is a high-stake example of a dynamic frequently found in many homes.

A low-stake example of the same premise, (minus the illegality), is a three-year-old who throws a huge fit at Target because she wants her parents to buy a plastic backyard swimming pool. If a child learns that throwing a tantrum is an option to use to get what she wants, she has just learned something she will have to unlearn later in life. If she learns that throwing a fit will *not* get her what she wants, she has learned a lesson that will serve her well over time.

SETBACKS AND ANTI-LEARNING

Anything we learn interpersonally, developmentally, spiritually, or academically that we will eventually have to unlearn in order to grow is a setback or *anti-learning*. Anti-learning is when we learn something that takes us further from the truth than just a neutral position.

A second grader might learn that hitting another child is the best way to be respected. A twenty-three-year-old might learn that if she drives slowly and carefully, she can drive home when she has had too much to drink. The pattern is the same with the second grader and the twenty-three-year-old. A bad decision is followed by a short-term gain, which leads to learning a false lesson. This anti-learning adds to the list of things that must be unlearned to move ahead.

Why spend time on this in a parenting book? Because we feel people of all ages are using maladaptive ways to get what they want, just like the dog on the couch. Every time we use maladaptive behavior to get what we want, it is a setback to growth. This has become an underlying issue in raising kids. Every time our kids learn something that will need to be unlearned, their progress has been slowed and postponed.

AA and other drug-and-alcohol treatment programs say little or no growth happens during the years that addicts use anything to alter their moods. A twenty-eight-year-old who has been using drugs for twelve years will likely act in many ways like a fifteen- or sixteen-year-old. Little significant growth happened during those twelve years of drug abuse.

Part of the reason for this could be anti-learning. In many areas of their lives, drug abusers have come up with the wrong answers to life's right questions. They will need to unlearn these answers. Almost every person who has ever used cocaine, crack, or heroin ends up wishing he or she had never touched the stuff. The lives of addicts may look completely different from each other and the length of time of their use may vary by decades. But, they all start at the same place. They use a maladaptive behavior, (drugs), to get what they want, (acceptance, peace, or euphoria). Each time they repeated the behavior, their false learning was reinforced. They may think, *this is enhancing my life and my fun.* In the end, they all end in the same place—realizing that it has nearly cost them everything they hold dear.

For a parent of a four-year-old, this story will seem hard to relate to and irrelevant. But, it isn't irrelevant. Replace the twenty-three-year-old girl with a four-year-old boy, her maladaptive use of drugs with his tantrum behaviors, and the common theme of this principle is apparent. The longer we as adults—or our children—use unhealthy, maladaptive behaviors to get our needs and wants met, the further anti-learning will take us from healthy living.

Unhealthy Learning

There is a fundamentally sound way to learn lasting lessons in life that results in maturity: *When I make a good choice, something good happens. When I make a bad choice, something bad happens.* Of course, there are numerous exceptions, but this is a primary way to learn. Unfortunately, distinguishing between good and bad is not always easy. We would learn much faster if it were.

Even more disruptive to the process is that we often make poor decisions that end up with a positive outcome. This sounds really simple but it isn't. Unfortunately, children of all ages consistently get what they want from a poor approach. It is important for parents to try to manage their households and children in a way that minimizes the frequency of children deriving a good outcome from negative behavior.

This dynamic is evident in the hundreds of conversations we have had with teenagers reflecting on their summer vacations. What they talk about as the "best night of the whole summer" is often the night they made the worst decisions of the entire summer. Perhaps they drank while underage, or used drugs, or took someone else's boat out without permission, or broke into a store or the local high school. This can happen at any age. Every time a child makes a poor decision without a cost, it is a setback for growth. Here are some examples:

- An eighth grader copies a quiz from the person next to him and gets his best score of the quarter.

- A tenth grader jumps in a lake with her cell phone in her pocket and her parents give her a new and better smartphone.

- A third grader screams that the family never goes anywhere fun. In response, the parents plan a trip to a theme park.

- An unpopular sixteen-year-old girl brings a bottle of vodka to a sleepover and is suddenly the center of attention.

- On his eighteenth birthday, a young man goes to a local casino and in forty minutes wins $1,800.

- A fifteen-year-old girl badgers her mother mercilessly when she is told she can't go to a sleepover where there are no parents home. Out of sheer exhaustion, her mother gives in with these infamous words: "Just this once."

- A five-year-old who was supposed to be in bed at 9 p.m. cries and kicks and convinces mom that she can't sleep and ends up in the master bedroom having a story read to her till 11:00 p.m.

- A bright and distracted fifteen-year-old who had played video games for a month straight, now finds himself five assignments behind in math. He screams at his parents that he needs to move out of high math and be put in a lower class. He accuses his parents of not understanding him and repeats over and over that they never "listen." The parents sign a form and the next Monday he has his first day in the lower math class.

There is nothing catastrophically wrong with any of these examples in and of themselves. But, all of these are examples of anti-learning. This means that what the child just learned is eventually going to have to be unlearned. Unfortunately, unlearning can be a long and painful process.

[Note: It's fine to read your child a story when she can't sleep if you want to; we have both done this on many occasions as dads. Just remember two things. First, inconsistent outcomes to your child's behavior do not create the best learning environment. And second, we need to have patience and compassion for our kids when they are learning slowly because of our sporadic or inconsistent responses to their behavior. We need to understand that we played a part in that delay.]

When a Poor Decision Pays Off

Almost all boys in their late teens or early twenties who have serious gambling problems report that they were "fortunate" enough to have huge winnings the first or second time at the casino, betting with a bookie, or at the horse track. Recreationally, a casino can be a fun and an exciting form of entertainment, but as a financial strategy it is a poor decision. In the end, the house wins. When the result of a young man's poor decision to try to get a windfall at the slots results in huge winnings, it is a good outcome from a poor decision. Many young men are hooked quickly and it may take years for them to realize that a casino is not a sound financial option. Even if a person wins one of their first times at a casino and rarely wins after that, it can take decades for him to unlearn his first experience at the slots.

The closest many of us ever come to winning at a casino is putting a five-dollar bill in a soda machine and listening to that sweet sound of $3.50 in quarters fall down into the change slot. If that is as good as my gambling luck has ever been, it isn't hard for you to see a casino as a bad investment.

It is important that parents learn to see when a poor decision is paying off for their child. Not for any great moral reason, but rather because growing up is a long enough process without the impact of "anti-learning." Whenever kids learn things that they are going to have to unlearn, the journey to maturity becomes risky and needlessly prolonged.

When kids break the law and police only give them a warning, some teens see this as a bad outcome. But more often kids see it as just a close call without a bad outcome for their poor choice. Well-meaning and reasonable police officers will break up parties and tolerate minor consumption with a "let-it-go-this-time" approach. This is not really being a friend to the kids who won't learn a lesson from a close call. For those kids it is anti-learning. Instead of facing the consequences of underage drinking, including a possible court date, they are learning that the police aren't that serious about upholding this particular law. This results in slowed and confused learning.

Mature learning takes good choices even further. It adds the concept of delayed gratification to the initial experience of immediate gratification. With delayed gratification, a significant part of making repeated good choices is that those choices will usually or *eventually* pay off. Good choices don't always pay off. If they do, it might not be immediately, but they are our best bet. Day after day, choosing to do homework, coming home on time, eating healthy, and saving money will usually and eventually pay off.

We don't want to teach kids to just be good rule followers. This is not the panacea we might think it is. But, we can support wisdom, responsibility, delayed gratification, and kindness when we see it, whether the rules were followed or not.

GOOD DECISIONS, BAD OUTCOMES

Setbacks can also take place when a child makes a good decision and has a bad outcome. This dynamic is frequently found in alcoholic homes, but can be seen anywhere. A responsible teen in a dysfunctional home who shows how responsible he is may be given more and more of the burden of the home. It is less prevalent in the gereral population, but common enough to mention. An oldest child can carry enormous weight on her shoulders and pay a high price throughout childhood for being so competent. This can make the child look highly responsible, but healthy learning is not occurring. These kids will often eventually rebel or act out when they see that being reliable is not gaining them anything they want in life. The bad outcome is more and more inappropriate responsibility as a result of being competent. Some of these kids hate conflict so much that they are willing to be over-responsible just to reduce tension in the home.

Parents seem to be confused about what is a good or a bad outcome. This confusion comes from a faulty way of seeing bad outcomes. They may see an outcome as bad because they themselves would interpret it as bad, but their child doesn't see it as bad. Some kids see conflict as a bad outcome and will alter their behavior to avoid conflict. Other kids love conflict and are energized by an argument. Even eye contact is a reward for young children. Looking at a child with a disapproving glare is not a bad outcome for some kids. It can actually be a reward.

Find out what is paying off for your child and what is costing him something. This is just as true with a three-year-old as it is with an eighteen-year-old. At any age, a parent should first see if they can get out of the way and let life handle the outcome. This should always be the first instinct. Life isn't always consistent in delivering appropriate outcomes. When that happens, parents need to redirect life to adjust the result.

If a child loses his baseball cap at a restaurant, nothing needs to be said or done about that. Life did its job. But, if a farm kid forgets to feed her horse one day, there is no natural cost to the child for this mistake. The parent then needs to steer the outcome. Otherwise, only the horse pays the price for the error.

PRODUCTIVE LEARNING

Productive learning is when a life lesson is learned cleanly and efficiently, without all the setbacks and interference that usually accompany a lesson. Anti-learning may be the biggest setback but, over-talking, excuses, inconsistency, and resentment all hinder productive learning.

To illustrate nearly perfect productive learning, we are going to use a fictional example for a couple of reasons. First, there just aren't very many perfect examples in real life because real life has a way of altering perfection. Second, we learn so fast from productive learning that we hardly even realize we have learned a lesson.

Imagine that a new law for teenage drivers requires a GPS device to be installed that would send real-time data to a law enforcement computer. This device would keep track of where a car is at all times as well as what the speed limit is where the vehicle is being driven. A computer would know exactly how fast the car was going in relation to the speed limit and that data would be analyzed and stored. This system would allow a moment or two of speeding for passing or on a downhill stretch of road. But, if the teen were speeding more than a minute or two, the computer would notify a chip in the car that too much time had been spent over the speed limit.

The GPS in the car would also know when the car was at home in the driveway. The chip would wait as long as needed for the car to get home and be shut off. Once the car was shut off, the chip in the car would send a message that the car would not start for twenty-four hours. After twenty-four hours, the car would return to normal operation.

This system, (apart from the problems and exceptions inherent with any fictional example), would stop nearly all teenage speeding in a matter of days. It would work so efficiently that, within a month, teenage speeding would be a thing of the past. Here are the reasons this lesson would be learned so thoroughly and rapidly.

- There is a positive outcome (driving) from a positive decision and a negative outcome (car won't start for twenty-four hours) from a negative decision.

- The law did not bring extraneous factors into the situation like grades or a messy room.

- There is no dialogue between the parents and teen. All that the parent needs to say is, "Oh, that is too bad; you can try it again tomorrow."

- The cost of speeding is significant but not punitive. Kids learn best from brief and costly consequences that aren't excessive.

- The rules apply to everyone, so a teen that is shut down doesn't feel singled out.

- There are no setbacks to learning since there is no one else to blame, no excuses, and no one with whom the teen can plead his case.

This type of productive learning, though seldom available to us in real life, illustrates how efficiently and completely a lesson is learned without anti-learning and the static interference that delays most learning situations.

The GIST of It

- The most efficient way to learn is to have a good outcome from a good choice, and a bad outcome from a bad choice. This is efficient learning because it avoids anti-learning; we avoid learning things we will need to unlearn at some time in the future.

- As a parent, be mindful of how your child learns. Try to help him or her learn the inevitable lessons of life as early as possible. Minimize the number of good outcomes your child has from poor decisions and try to make sure that their best decisions result in something positive.

- A household that resembles the way life really works is one where it is taught that there is not always a good outcome from a good decision but, over time it is our best bet.

- Make sure your child is not having bad outcomes for performing well.

Chapter Three:

The Nature of Life

L ife is the teacher best qualified to prepare us for living. But, if we aren't paying attention, it is easy to block life's lessons from our kids and ourselves. If we miss these lessons of life we will prevent our children from being *life-ready*.

It's hard to know how life-ready someone may be, but easy to see when he is not.

A twenty-something young adult who can't manage his money, apply himself in college, or get himself out of bed in the morning is not life-ready. This may be due to a lack of focus in the family on the nature of life. Sometimes there are learning disabilities and other reasons for this delay, but usually it is just that the family system does not think in terms of kids being life-ready.

Innumerable things go right in this world—thank goodness. These are not things we need to prepare for, so they don't require much attention. But, there are things that can go wrong in life, and there are skills needed to handle those things when they go wrong. Our kids need to be preparing for the times when life kicks back.

When experienced campers spend weeks preparing for a trip into the wilderness, most of their prep time is for the moments where something could go wrong. There isn't a lot of prep needed for a warm, sunny day with a light breeze out of the southwest. They are preparing for the circumstances that can go wrong on a journey. The better prepared they are for difficult situations, the better the trip will go.

We have collected what we believe to be the six most necessary perspectives for living a well-functioning life. Though there are thousands of lessons to learn, usually these six will keep young adults from imminent danger in those early years of adulthood.

These six life lessons are: accepting that life is difficult, developing self-discipline, being resilient, acquiring age-appropriate relationship skills, experiencing personal achievement, and understanding that both hope and pain are necessary parts of growing.

The backbone of our parenting philosophy is that the job of parents is to prepare their kids for life. Not counting years one through three, we have about seventeen years to give our kids some kind of view of how life works and enough practice runs for them to develop life skills. We suspect there is not a lot of disagreement about this goal. Yet, why are a huge percentage of kids not life-ready when they turn twenty?

#1. Life is Difficult

Many people seem to have misperceived the nature of living. The true nature of life has always been that it is difficult. Many in our culture may not believe this truth, and many children are not being taught this reality. People who have not internalized this are not hard to identify. These are the ones who complain when normal obstacles and disappointments converge on their lives. They feel as if life is unfair and they proclaim this injustice repeatedly. From the outside looking in, people who don't accept that life is difficult, seem to be tormented by normalcy.

Our kids need to know the truth. In an easy life, tires still go flat, cars don't start, zippers break, gift cards are lost, connections are missed, and phones go dead. In a normal life you can expect to lose a job, be unable to pay your bills, have a serious illness in your family, experience a divorce, have parents with dementia, or lose property in a storm.

Young people may be shocked at the inequity of it all if their lives are not going smoothly. If you own a house on a flood plain, you should not feel outraged when the water occasionally rises too high. Don't be bewildered by debt if you take out six years of school loans. Expect to ruin your transmission if you repeatedly squeal your tires. The tragedy in these examples is not the flooded basement, the debt, or the transmission. The tragedy is when people lose hope because they didn't think life would be this difficult. This is a lesson they needed to learn earlier.

I have never in my life envied a human being who led an easy life. I have envied a great many people who led difficult lives and led them well.

- Theodore Roosevelt

Relatively few people get by with an easy life. Even people who say they have an easy life often mean it could be worse than it is. Music superstars, famous actors, great athletes, even kings and queens often have tremendous difficulties in life.

"Life is difficult," M. Scott Peck wrote in his groundbreaking bestseller, *The Road Less Traveled*. Peck argued that the problems many people face come from the failure to accept the truth that life is difficult. He said, "This is a great truth, one of the greatest truths. It is a great truth because once we truly see this truth, we transcend it. Once we truly know that life is difficult—once we truly understand and accept it—then life is no longer difficult. Because once it is accepted, the fact that life is difficult no longer matters."

A glance back at the previous thirty generations shows us that much of life consisted of problems, and much of living was solving those problems. This has never changed and it never will change. There was the occasional dance, holiday, birthday party, swimming hole, or harvest celebration. But, for the most part, life was a struggle to solve one problem after another just to stay alive.

Fifty years ago no one had trouble with the cable guy, no one was the victim of identity theft, no one lost his entire music library when a friend pushed him into a swimming pool, and no one had a fit when they missed the 4:00 p.m. deadline for next-day delivery.

A few hundred years ago a young woman would be aware that, if she were going to have two children survive to adulthood, she would likely need to bear three or four children. That was a given and, in a way, was accepted. Those were difficult times, in some ways, terrible times. But, life was made easier because very few people dreamed of having it easy.

Life is not a spectacle or a feast. It is a predicament.

- George Santayana

When we don't accept the truth that life is difficult we wonder what we or someone else did wrong for life not to go smoothly. We use self-blame, blaming others, blaming God, or denial to try to explain to ourselves why things are going wrong in a life where things are *supposed* to go right.

Try hosting Thanksgiving at your house with the goal of having the day turn out perfectly. Compare that approach to hosting Thanksgiving recognizing that difficulty is pretty much inevitable. Flaws don't matter that much when we accept that everything can't go perfectly. There is less stress, less blaming of self and others, and less denial.

Feeding a family is difficult. Going to school is difficult. Playing a sport is difficult. Relationships are difficult. Injuries are difficult. Dating can be difficult. Even owning a dog can be difficult. The more we fail to accept that difficulty is inherent in life, the more we will struggle, blame, medicate, and feel depressed and overwhelmed. Anger and frustration are often indicators that we believe our lives should go smoothly. An angry person is often someone who has not accepted this truth.

While life will always be difficult, it is not constantly difficult. There are periods of time, sometimes years and sometimes decades, in which we are spared serious difficulty. Whether anticipated or not, some hardship touches most people eventually. There is no amount of wealth, faith, education, or health that can keep people immune from these trials.

Anger and frustration are indicators that we believe life should go smoothly.

Those who have not yet faced some type of tragedy in their lives, or perhaps haven't had one in decades, may start to believe that they are exempt from the struggles that others face. They might believe that they know how to build a start-up company, or they know how to avoid a heart attack, or even raise perfect kids. They may feel that they have solved life's problems or they are being spared these hardships. Something humbling is often in their future. These are the people that say, "Three years ago I never dreamed I would be in this situation." When tragedy comes, they experience a collision between their hopes and the reality of their lives.

While some lives may look blessed for a time, very few people avoid the experiences of feeling lost, confounded, or strained. We need to tell kids that this universal truth is the nature of life. It will not serve children well to grow up believing that a problem-free life is the goal—or even an option. To enjoy life in the long term, our best hope is to learn to enjoy problem solving.

THE REAL NORMAL

A random group of men met one weekend at a men's conference in Colorado. Nothing in particular brought them together other than the fact that they were all men. By national standards, these men could easily have been seen as having good lives because most were employed, healthy, educated, and successful.

The talks and events of the weekend were designed only to get the men to open up and talk about things they typically didn't talk about. The agenda steered the men toward being real and nothing more: just talking about what life had been like for them.

As the men started to talk, a hushed silence fell over the group. Smartphones were put away and no one was daydreaming or distracted. As each man took a turn awkwardly sharing the narrative of his life, the others seemed riveted by the stories being told. After half of the men had revealed their perhaps previously untold stories, a man sitting near one of the leaders leaned over and asked, "Were these men all hand-picked or screened ahead of time? How is it that you gathered so many men together who all had so much pain and disappointment in their lives?" The leader pondered this question knowing there had been no screening. All of these men had taken a shot at living life—that was all.

If you've been living a while and are engaged in life, chances are you will be exposed to more pain or sadness than you anticipated. It's a myth that we all deserve relatively problem-free lives. As a culture, we are quickly moving toward a mindset that reinforces the belief that little or nothing should go wrong in life. We are led to believe that after retirement or a divorce we should be able to maintain the lifestyle to which we have grown accustomed. We start out believing that our children will grow up healthy. Autism will be something the neighbor in the green house has to deal with. Our kids won't struggle with sexual identity or deal drugs or carry some potentially terminal illness.

It is astounding to see the extent to which we believe we should not have to struggle. We hear, "I never thought that *this* (you fill in the blank), would happen to me." We seem to believe we shouldn't get fired, lose a season ticket lottery, have hypertension, miss our flight connections, get food poisoning, or be shorted in an estate settlement. Our kids should be at least above average and they shouldn't be inadequate or ungifted in any way.

In one collision after another, life reminds us how false these myths are. Life is more difficult than we are led to expect. Through painful life events we learn that a trouble-free life is rare at best. Few have suffered like the fictional character Fantine in *Les Miserables*. But, when she sings, "now life has killed the dream I dream," tears flood faces in the audience. People relate to this universal theme: life is harder than they expected.

To raise life-ready kids, teach them the lesson that life is difficult. This is not bad news. It is just the nature of life and we need to accept this.

#2. Developing Self-Discipline

Once we have accepted that life will always present problems, the next skill is to solve those problems. Solving problems requires facing problems. The most effective way to face problems is by using self-discipline.

Nothing can truly take the place of discipline in life, although our culture has taken its shots at trying to find a replacement. Some hope that grace can be a replacement for discipline. They try to solve their problems by letting themselves off the hook or finding someone else to solve their problems. Perhaps they hope that, without the weight of guilt or the burden of failure, they will just naturally face the challenges of life better. That might be an appealing thought, but it is simply not reality. We all need moments of grace from time to time; however, if grace is too often dispensed it slows the process of developing self-discipline.

Discipline is as different from self-discipline as others-esteem is from self-esteem. Both are needed in life but they are not the same. Sometimes discipline evolves into self-discipline and sometimes it doesn't. This is important for parents to remember. The primary intention for instilling discipline in our kids is that it will, hopefully, evolve into self-discipline.

Let's distinguish between discipline and the self-discipline we hope our kids will have learned by the time they are twenty-one. Discipline can be thought of as external motivations we use to make good choices, usually from an authority figure. The hope is that necessary motivations will be internalized into self-discipline. Discipline that never makes this transformation to self-discipline is good, but has limited value. Not all parenting approaches are conducive to facilitating this transition. Some parenting strategies are far more likely to develop self-discipline in our kids. These kinds of interventions should be used predominantly.

The degree and frequency of college freshmen struggling and failing in their first year away from home indicates that too often the transition to self-discipline isn't happening. Discipline may motivate an eighteen-year-old girl to keep her room straight and get a reasonable night's sleep when she is home. But, if her primary motivation in doing so is others-centered—"I don't want to make Mom mad" or "I don't want to have my parents ground me"—this hasn't evolved into self-discipline. In that case, her dorm room will likely be a disaster and she might be staying up half the night. This is an example of a situation where the transition would not yet have occurred.

The evolution from discipline to self-discipline is not automatic. It is something that needs to occur in all of us, even into adulthood. Self-discipline often involves conforming to an internal motivation, while discipline usually involves complying with an external motivation. This, in part, explains why the development of self-discipline needs to evolve. We start learning something with the benefit of an outside influence and finish learning it when we have made it our own.

A traveler may pack lightly for a trip or two because of a luggage limit set by a tour company. Then, a few years later she may pack lightly because she has learned the burden of hauling too many belongings around on a trip.

The road to self-discipline may be a relatively direct route, but can be painfully circuitous. How we parent and how we talk will influence how long this journey is, but it will never eliminate the journey completely. Parents who are aware of this progression will watch and value this shift when they see it. Creativity is needed to assist kids as they transform discipline to self-discipline.

Scolding children for leaving belongings in the family room might get them to put their things away (though it is doubtful). But, this approach will rarely result in self-discipline. In contrast, quietly dumping a child's belongings in a large designated box in the garage without a word is more likely to promote self-discipline. This will become personal for our kids when they are inconvenienced enough by digging through three bushels of junk to find an item they left out. The child's thinking process will develop from "I pick up after myself so Dad won't be mad" to "I pick up after myself because I don't want to dig through the box again." Letting consequences teach the child is more likely to result in the development of self-discipline.

Self-discipline is our friend. It plays a more important role in our lives and in our role as parents than just being obedient. Without this, we will be lost and ill equipped for life. While all discipline can help prepare us for life, it is self-discipline that provides the greatest tools for handling life's difficulties.

#3. Resilience

You had better be ready for failure if you hope to be ready for life. Failure is a part of life. Resilience is what separates failure from defeat. When we fall, we need to get back up. Anyone wanting to be ready to face life will need an ample supply of resilience.

We all need the ability to handle disappointment. Thousands of entrepreneurs do not succeed until their fourth or fifth idea. Many physicians did not get into the medical school they wanted, but they got in somewhere. Great athletes blow out their knees. Perhaps most painful, some have the love of their life reject them and walk away unconcerned with the pain they have left behind. Preparing our children for life is preparing them to pick themselves up, dust themselves off, and try again—the next time with greater humility and determination.

Resilience is what separates failure from defeat.

Many kids today have an easy life and they don't even know it. Some think losing a smartphone for a couple of days is hardship. Unless children have been exposed to an event that puts their struggles in perspective, they may lose their balance over minor inconveniences in life.

One of the problems is that many parents do not want their kids to have a rough time in life. They want their kids to have fun, fit in, and not have to struggle. It might make for a pleasant appearing childhood to overly accommodate a son or daughter, but it runs a huge risk of leaving that child unprepared for adulthood. We have never seen adolescents thrive when they are living life their way. Left to their own devices kids care little if they are solving a problem, delaying a problem, dumping a problem on someone else, or medicating a problem.

They need the struggle. They need disappointment. They need limits. They need something to push against to become strong. And this must be done in a way where the struggle is against life and not against us as parents.

Resilience is essential to life. When the annual NCAA basketball tournament called March Madness starts, it is a given that sixty-three of the sixty-four best basketball teams in the country will end their season with a loss. We experience lost papers, lost love, lost freedom, lost purpose, lost health, lost pets, and lost reputations.

So much of resilience is perception. Your child may need help assessing not only the magnitude of the difficulty he experiences, but also the degree to which he should express his emotional response. Consistent and accurate feedback as to how much an event should or should not disappoint him will help a child have a mature grid by which to develop resilience.

Children of all ages need help in assessing the magnitude of a difficulty. Small children do not know inherently how afraid they should be of a tornado. When they hear a funnel is in the area they may look into their father's eyes, listen to his tone of voice and his words and from that, determine the magnitude of the risk. Without knowing it, the dad is developing the child's spectrum of risk. Likewise, we need to help our children develop a spectrum of difficulty. Consistent and accurate feedback on how big a disappointment is will help a child develop an assessment grid for disappointments and struggles.

"Isn't that over-controlling your kids' emotions? Shouldn't they feel free to feel whatever they want?" Our answer is "No." A child's feelings are not just his own. They affect the whole family and are often not based on rationality. His feelings are just the intersection of his beliefs and his reality. You cannot control what your child feels, but you can and should comment on those reactions derived from a distorted belief.

If a ten-year-old boy cries, screams about an injustice, and no longer wants his friends over because his video game controller broke, he needs some help putting this disappointment into perspective. He needs help recalibrating the event. Perhaps, he needs to be told that this is a mild disappointment as disappointments go in life. Over time, this will immensely help his resilience.

Kids who are not well adjusted to disappointment will not be resilient. Don't protect your children from disappointments. Let them face them at age-appropriate levels as they grow. More importantly, dispel the myth that everything should go well. That way your children will at least not be surprised when they are confronted with challenges later in life.

When Our Balloons Pop

Steve and Anne had two young daughters who particularly loved helium balloons and their capricious ability to defy gravity. If the girls asked for balloons at a fair or a carnival, sometimes Steve would buy them and sometimes he wouldn't. When he did buy them, he'd always remind the girls before the purchase, "Now remember, every balloon has a sad ending. If we buy you balloons we want you to remember that the balloons don't tend to end well." Steve was right. Balloons don't end well. They pop, shrivel, or they are accidentally released and float off into the clouds. On the disappointment scale, the loss of a balloon is miniscule. Steve and Anne were aware that the girls would soon and invariably lose what they received. They wanted the girls to be aware of that truth too.

When I heard this story, I was impressed by the acceptance and resolve with which the daughters both handled the untimely demise of their balloons. Yet, I wasn't surprised. Just knowing that some form of disappointment would follow the purchase seemed to equip the girls better for the inevitable. Like all of us, they were emotionally able to better handle the loss by knowing the risks going in.

Kids should be told that the family's cocker spaniel has a typical life span of twelve years and that Shaggy is already seven years old now. The teenage boy should be told that the pickup truck he wants to buy may need a new transmission fairly soon. Parents should tell their daughter that her new basketball coach tends to belittle his players, so she shouldn't be surprised if he embarrasses her in front of the team.

These are simple ways of teaching and reminding kids that they can expect life to be tough, but that you believe they are just as tough and will be able to handle most anything thrown their way.

Losing a balloon is essentially a non-event, so this true story best serves as a metaphor. If we recognize that life is difficult and unfair we, and our kids, will be better able to face problems when they arise. We'll also enjoy life more during the good or easy times. How many times have we all heard someone with a serious illness say, "I will never take my health for granted again"? When we expect an easy life or a healthy life we take it for granted. We don't savor the joys of life as much.

Steve and Anne taught their girls a resilient way of looking at life:

- They knew balloons burst,

- They were better prepared to handle disappointment, and

- They appreciated the balloons more as they didn't take them for granted.

#4. Relationship Skills

Relationships are essential to every aspect of life and are a huge part of what makes life meaningful. Kids need to develop as many skills as they can for the myriad of relationship situations life will throw at them. Family, school, job, and sports all involve relationships. None of us would want to do adulthood without relationships. And, none of us can do relationships without some highly developed skills. To be good at relationships, there are certain skills that are essential: forgiveness, the ability to receive and give a gift, loving, caring for, listening to, trusting, and being honest.

How do we help our kids develop these relationship skills? Demanding that a child, "say you're sorry to your brother" will not develop a child who is sorry he hit his brother. No, there is a more difficult lesson to be learned than that. As in all relationship skills, it involves being able to put himself in another person's perspective and pausing a moment to imagine what life would feel like if it were happening to him.

Until age eight, it is normal and appropriate for a child to be egocentric. He views everything in relation to himself, is self-centered, and feels the effect that an event has on him. After eight, a child needs to develop the skill of seeing things from someone else's point of view. It is a lesson to be learned in the second half of childhood. To feel empathy for someone else's sorrow or struggle is the essence of compassion. Kids are not all born with this capacity; it needs to be developed. Compassion is actually a skill that can be cultivated and strengthened.

If your son is ten or older and still can't see aspects of life from another person's perspective, you need to give this some attention. Ask your son to tell you what he imagines the neighbor boy feels like now that his parents are getting a divorce or after his dog has died. You can talk with your son and ask him to imagine this before he goes over to his friend's house for the day. Throughout his lifetime he will use this ability to keep healthy relationships.

The digital age and social media have added new challenges in developing relationship skills for adults, but especially for kids. The digital shorthand we are all exposed to is convenient and quick, but there are aspects of socialization and interpersonal skills that are clearly being bypassed. Unfortunately, social media is uniquely designed for a sort of *touch-poin*t type of communication. It doesn't foster relationships with all the nuances and complexities that relationships require.

Texts and Twitter and Facebook posts, as well as e-mail, tend to be short conveyances of data. They are almost like the communication style from twenty years ago of leaving Post-It Notes all over an apartment to communicate with a friend or roommate. This form of contact connects but doesn't really relate. In essence, young people are connecting more frequently than ever before and relating less.

Social media is uniquely designed for touch-point communication but doesn't foster relationships.

There is a difference between a boy texting his boss that he is going to be ten minutes late for work versus calling his boss to tell her that he is running late or, before cell phones, arriving late and looking her in the eye and explaining why he was late. Texting and voicemails are emotional shortcuts. E-mailing the neighbor to say you can't mow his lawn this week is different than telling the neighbor the same thing in person. All of these examples are insignificant on their own. However, when these touch-point communications are pervasive and there is no human interaction, some important skills and reality are bypassed.

Consider the same dynamic in emotionally charged situations. We have all heard stories of kids starting a dating relationship with a text and then breaking up with another text. This is connection without texture. Birthday wishes, sympathy expressions and condolences after a death, congratulation for a graduation, and get-well wishes are now often done in touch points. These connections are more prevalent than ever. While Facebook users typically receive more birthday wishes now than they ever have, there is also less depth and fewer nuances to these wishes.

To have successful relationships, dozens of unique skills are needed. All need to be at least partially developed during childhood.

#5. Experiencing Achievement and Creativity

Achievement and creativity are often underplayed as an important part of personal development. It is from achievement that hope evolves into self-esteem. Without achievement, hope never evolves past being a wish. Kids who try to like themselves without achievement find it a hollow and hopeless journey. But to achieve or create, a price must be paid. If we want to run a marathon, write a paper or a song, earn a degree, or hunt a deer, an effort must be invested for that achievement. Adulthood involves accepting this truth and paying the price.

People do everything from camping to cross-country skiing to Sudoku and crossword puzzles for recreation. Some people will spend years fixing up an old Camaro or building deck furniture. Others enjoy golf, which is essentially one problem after another. People enjoy doing hobbies because they have found a focus where achievement is fun.

Hope evolves into self-esteem from achievement. Without achievement, hope never gets past wishing.

Achieving level four on a video game is a form of achievement. Ironically, since the game is a virtual battle, it is a virtual achievement. Having 500 Facebook friends may seem like an achievement to a child, but it really means they added hundreds of people they don't know. Perhaps the real achievement would be to have thirty Facebook friends. Landing a plane using a flight simulator is not like landing a real plane on a real runway. While it may develop some skill, there is no real risk.

To turn the corner into adulthood, young people need real achievement for a real world. Without real achievement, growth tends to dissipate and the hope and competence longed for is not produced.

When parents or social workers try to help kids who have lost their way, one of the hardest hurdles is to find that first significant achievement on which the child can build. It may sound easy, but it isn't. Parents frequently discover themselves in this predicament. If a child spends years never following through on anything, he will gradually find he has no tangible achievements. If a teenager spends years smoking pot, playing video games, breaking friendships, losing assignments, and having poorly developed social skills, he will end up with nothing that qualifies as a legitimate accomplishment. This is a problem.

In our respective practices we have heard kids list their latest achievements as hanging out at the mall and getting a tattoo. Getting to level six on a video game or exceeding 500 Facebook friends are sometimes called achievements. These are not achievements. Parents should remind their children these are games, events, purchases, or pleasures. An achievement is something totally different.

Nicole's Story

When Nicole was placed in a foster home she had achieved virtually nothing that could be called an accomplishment in years. With her truancy record she hadn't even accomplished going to school or turning in any assignments, let alone passing a grade. She had no real friends, no identifiable skills, and a limited ability to relate to people.

As she reluctantly got in her new foster family's van, Nicole complained. Going anywhere in the van with this family was a bona fide nightmare to her. Even worse, the family was going to "the cabin." To her, the cabin was nothing more than a small, congested shack in the middle of nowhere. She hated everything about it.

On her third day there, out of boredom, Nicole agreed to go out in a fishing boat. An hour later, with her negative attitude, no patience, and an awful cast, she somehow hooked an eight-pound northern pike. Even more unlikely, she was able to land the fish safely.

As the boat pulled up to the dock the family stopped what they were doing and ran for their cameras, shocked to see the transformation of Nicole's body language and the appearance of her smile. She wouldn't hold her own fish, but she was happy to stand near while cameras and smartphones clicked away. Nicole whispered quietly but clearly, "I'm so proud of myself." When she saw everyone seemed comfortable with this shy utterance, she said it again and again—louder and louder.

Four hours later, the fish had been cleaned and prepared and was more than enough to feed the family and a guest with leftovers. By this time, Nicole had left her frown and her timidity behind and was nearly yelling, "I'm so proud of myself" over and over again. She had finally stumbled onto an achievement on which she could start building.

Achievement is often the first step in any child's journey to heal or build self-esteem.

#6. Hope and Pain

Kids learn and grow when they have a combination of hope and pain in their lives. They usually need both. This means that an adolescent who has no pain will likely not mature. Likewise, a teen with no hope will not grow. Kids like Nicole have enough pain to grow, but their hope has dissipated along the way and they have nothing left on which to build successes.

Hope and pain are the nature of life. Call it struggle, difficulty, or challenge, but for ground to be fertile for growth, hope and pain usually need to be present. Life can't be too easy or too dark. Growth in a child slows down if pain and hope are not balanced. To jump-start growth, keep an eye on what part of this balance needs to be adjusted.

This is an important thing for parents and youth professionals to keep in mind. Many youth camps today have a ropes course, a zip-line, or some other apparatus that creates this combination. A twenty-five foot high rope to cross provides the fear or pain to face and peers cheering them on provides the hope.

How this happens is not always clear—it is not a science. For Nicole, catching a big fish was clearly hope. It wasn't planned out to work that way; the family just went fishing. After that, Nicole had an achievement and several photos for her Facebook page to build on. There was a chance for her next activity to also become an achievement.

Exposure to struggle and hope is not easily arranged or contrived. Often life presents challenges and anticipation in its own natural way. Some children will have this natural balance in their lives. A young child who falls off a skateboard or horse without serious injury will instinctively balance the fall with the adding of a new skill. An older teen might find this balance by trying out for a school play or waiting tables at a restaurant.

Too often an equal balance of hope and pain is lacking in a child's life. Parents can add a challenge or add hopefulness as needed to partially orchestrate pain and hope in a child's life to achieve a reasonable balance.

The GIST of It

- If our kids are going to be ready for adulthood by age twenty, they will need to accept that life is difficult.

- The more we accept that life will be a struggle, the less difficult it becomes.

- The healthiest approach for solving problems in life is self-discipline.

- Creativity, self-control, and a disciplined life are the best tools to solve most of life's inherent problems.

- Resilience allows us to try several times to correct a problem and provides the strength to get up when we have been knocked down.

- Resilience can only be strengthened through practice.

- We cannot go through life alone, so it is imperative that we learn relationship skills.

- Everyone proficient at life can get along with others.

- Compassion is essential to being a good friend and family member.

- Growth will not likely take place without a sense of achievement.

Chapter Four:
The Difference Between Fun and Joy

"**I** didn't have any fun today," is a complaint we've heard from the children and teens we see in our practices. The comment seems simple enough and yet, on closer examination, it grows complex. Whether spoken indignantly or with contempt, when a child says this, it reveals implications and assumptions about his or her cultural and worldview.

First, this simple statement implies that the child believes fun is something that *should be* part of his experience every day. It doesn't matter if he had fun yesterday. The issue is the irrefutable fact that he had no fun today.

Second, the complaint, "I didn't have any fun today," spoken in the tone that conveys that this *should not have happened*, reveals a deep-seated belief that a child has a fundamental right to daily fun. The baseline has shifted on this in recent years and some kids have come to assume that fun is an inherent entitlement, every day.

Third, the comment "I didn't have any fun today," implies it was *someone else's duty* to make this happen. While kids are aware that the lack of fun is not a form of neglect, they can see it as an injustice. It is as though they are saying, "Now look what you've done! You've blown it! You have contributed to a day of my life in which fun did not exist. It isn't fair that you did that to me!"

Perhaps more alarming is the number of times a parent takes on the weight of these assumptions. Usually this happens subconsciously. But, if a parent hears, "I didn't have any fun today," and feels guilty or feels like she failed, she has unwittingly, and perhaps accidentally, given in to this silent shift in our culture.

As fun gains prominence, joy dwindles.

Most parents would be aghast at feeding their children only chips, soda pop, and dessert. They're constantly aware of the impact of the child's diet on his health, self-image, energy, and future. These same parents will allow their children's lives to be dominated by fun activities, rather than meaningful activities that build joy. As fun gains prominence in our culture, joy dwindles in many children's lives.

Kids have a pretty good idea of what would be fun for them to do. In contrast, most kids we have met know little about what would give them joy.

Let's look at the definition of fun and joy as we use them in this chapter. The words fun and joy are not synonymous. Almost universally, people *sense* that there is a huge difference between fun and joy. Imagine saying to someone in parting, "Have joy," instead of saying, "Have fun." What a different meaning that would have! These two words cannot be interchanged, because they do not represent the same idea. Fun and joy are different in character, in form, in content and, above all, in intent.

Fun is morally indifferent and spiritually detached. Joy is morally grounded and spiritually aware. Fun has a bent toward excitement, while joy has a bent toward peace. Fun is enjoyable but often fleeting. Joy is far more enduring. There is a sense of meaning in joy. There is depth, gratitude, or perhaps wonder. It tends to remind us that life is worthwhile in a way that fun cannot.

WHAT'S WRONG WITH A LITTLE FUN?

This high priority on having fun is a huge shift from past generations. Among western youth there is a goal or even an expectation they should be entertained nearly every day. Little wonder entertainment is no longer something saved for special festivals, holidays, or weekends. "Let's have fun!" The prevailing thought is: *What's wrong with it? Life is short. Have fun, live a little, be good to yourself!*

For many kids the pursuit of fun has become a primary focus. Teens say the word "fun" more than almost any other. Having fun is a highly valued and popular goal. When kids part from each other or end a phone call, very often they'll give this message: "Have fun; don't work too hard."

Teens often talk together about how much fun they had at an activity or event. We suspect that if they were asked, "Did you experience any joy?" the typical response would be, "Joy? What do you mean? I just had fun."

Any form of escape inherently does not endure.

Young children grow and learn from play and fun activities. But, as a child hits his early teens, he should move from fun-dominated activities toward those with the potential to build joy.

Fun and joy are different in nature. Almost everyone is in favor of kids having fun and hardly anyone is against it. But, why should we have fun? The answer is, "Because it's fun!" Fun has become its own justification.

Fun has a fleeting and momentary nature. It expires in three hours or fifteen minutes after a great comedy movie or the morning after an amazing party. The pursuit process starts again as the person experiencing the fun returns to his life before the movie or the party. The movie was a two-hour escape and this may be all we are looking for, but an escape inherently does not endure. It is entertaining or funny or crazy or suspenseful and then it is over and nothing has changed. More importantly, we haven't changed anything in our world.

In our teen culture, kids are compensating for the fleeting nature of fun by pursuing it relentlessly. With such a short expiration date on fun, it must be purchased anew over and over. Fun used to be a wonderful seasoning for life. For some, it has become the main course. It was never meant to be the whole meal. As the main driving force of life, it is not very attractive.

Fun is a wonderful seasoning for life, but not the whole meal.

Fun has become mainstream as a value. There are a few coaches and mentors who challenge fun as a valued outcome, but they seem few and far between. Likewise, there are few books, sermons, speakers, or advertising that dare step into that murky air of challenging the merits of fun.

Many adults have bought into this personal movement. For these adults, chasing fun becomes a goal and a preoccupation. Fortunately, the responsibilities and commitments of most adults don't allow them to succumb to this. Others find it not as satisfying as they would hope. But, we've all seen adults who have become chasers of fun and live lives that resemble an extended and unattractive mid-life crisis.

Joy, on the other hand, is far more enduring. It doesn't show up as easily as fun but joy reminds us that life is worthwhile in a way that fun doesn't. There is not much fun in being honest, or in hard work, and little fun at all in self-discipline. What fun is there in being a kind grandson, a good sibling, or a young man of your word? What is fun about being grateful for what you have, or sacrificing for someone with less? Not very much fun.

The Benefits of Pursuing Joy

Why pursue joy? Because joy is more peace-filled and enduring than fun. Those who pursue joy don't have dull or uninteresting lives. They just value joy more than fun. Joy usually costs a little more and lasts a lot longer, and will give experiences that a focus on fun will never produce.

If someone is relentlessly pursuing fun, he might not be giving much thought to joy. This is not a conscious trade-off. He is simply unclear about the differences between them and what it is he really wants. It is common for someone to pursue fun when it may be joy that he really desires. Joy tends to cultivate a depth to life and a sturdier form of happiness that fun cannot produce.

Fun-focused kids rarely experience the happiness that comes from real joy. Serving at a food pantry during the holidays may not seem fun or exciting or even convenient. Yet, something happens in a child's heart when he sees tears well up in a woman's eyes as she smiles and says, "Thank you so much!

This will change the holidays for my family!" How about cutting into an afternoon of fun by cooking a meal with your child to take to a sick neighbor? Often we overlook or discount the joy that time spent in meaningful activity with our kids can bring.

Joyful activities don't need to be focused on someone else, but they do require some kind of investment. They can be completely selfish. Participating in *Tough Mudder*, or even losing thirty pounds can bring joy and these are self-serving events. A real adventure requires a real investment and usually produces joy. An artificial or counterfeit adventure, which is what all video games are, brings only fun.

Young people are inherently drawn to adventure. Girls and boys alike are instinctively drawn to heroes, competition, and challenges. If they aren't allowed or encouraged to pay the price of a real adventure, they will likely substitute it with virtual adventure or a fabricated drama. This counterfeit adventure will not satisfy their yearning and will bring only fun at best, and perhaps not even that.

IS FUN A PARENT'S RESPONSIBILITY?

We see an increasing number of parents who have taken on the weight of this shift in our culture. They feel the responsibility for helping their kids have fun and facilitating its endless pursuit. Some parents have bought into the notion that fun should be expected and frequent. Some parents even feel guilty if they haven't provided a steady diet of fun for their kids. They try to present fun options on a regular basis, feeling that this is part of the job description of a modern parent. Consciously or subconsciously, the progression sounds something like this in the parent's head:

- I love my child,

- I want my kids to have a happy childhood,

- My kids seem to need fun regularly to be happy,

- My younger kids have trouble coming up on their own with ways to have fun,

- If I interfere with my teenager's fun, I will interfere with his happiness, and

- My children have enough challenges in life so I need to facilitate their fun.

If we as parents mentor our children's fun, we will mentor them into a repeated chase and endless pursuit. These kids wonder as soon as they wake up: "What are we doing for fun today?" Because fun is by nature brief, kids schooled in fun will want to find it every day of the week. If we mentor our children in joy, we teach them to find something that has meaning and depth and something that is more enduring.

Here are some thoughts that consciously or subconsciously can help parents re-think this shift in our culture:

- Fun is fine, but joy is deeper and less fleeting.

- Joy usually requires creativity, achievement, self-discipline, or effort.

- Creativity is often birthed from passion, sacrifice, or boredom.

- Creativity or passion often leads to achievement.

- When my child finds joy in something, it will last a while and will contribute to his self-esteem.

Ironically, searching for fun can be an accomplishment that brings joy. This is why there is immense value in having young children discover their own fun. They find joy in the process of looking for fun. This is the primary difference between setting a child up with a game or fun activity, and patiently waiting for him to discover or invent an activity to play. When parents constantly find fun for their child, they are *stealing* the opportunity for the child to find joy in his own pursuit of fun. Be patient—creativity is often birthed from boredom.

Sarah's Story

Sarah was fifteen and very excited about going to Disney World. She was not too old nor too cool to enjoy a family vacation. She had wanted to go about three years ago, when her family had first talked about it. But, each spring either money or time was in short supply. This year Sarah's little brother was seven and old enough to enjoy the Disney experience along with another sister in the middle.

This was to be a once-in-a-lifetime trip and had taken much effort and time to pull together. The kids had spring breaks a week apart. The parents coincided the trip dates with the seven-year-old boy's vacation time. Sarah would miss a week of school and have four days left of vacation after they arrived home.

Their eight-day-trip included: Magic Kingdom, Sea World Orlando, Busch Gardens Tampa Bay, Universal Studios Florida, Discovery Cove, and Epcot. Plus the family was going to stay at one of the Walt Disney World Resorts. Sheer stamina may have been the biggest obstacle to perfection. But, the week went wonderfully and actually exceeded the family's lofty expectations.

Sarah and her family got home early on a Monday night, and Sarah went to bed that night reveling in the fact that she didn't have school the next morning. *How great was that?*

Tuesday morning all the family except Sarah kicked into function mode and dispersed to the individual demands of a normal week. Sarah slept in and didn't roll out of bed until nearly 11:00 a.m. She promptly found something to eat in the fridge, and checked to see if there was anything good on TV. There wasn't, so she settled into a casual Facebook update.

At 2:30 p.m., Sarah's mom got a text from Sarah. It didn't say, "Mom, thanks for the amazing vacation!" It didn't say, "Mom, I'm exhausted from seeing the best theme parks in the western hemisphere in one week." It didn't even say, "It's nice to be home." No, her short and to-the-point text simply read, "I'm bored. There's nothing fun to do here."

A Word about Truths

Joy is often richer than fun -- this is the truth captured in this chapter. The wonder of truths is that they can be signposts to help us navigate through life. Truths are guides proven over time to help us know whether to turn left or right when we get to the next fork in the road. Advice tells us what to do in a situation whereas truths give us a foundation to advise ourselves.

Too often these truths are not passed down to our kids. Perhaps this happens, in part, because there are always exceptions to a truth and these exceptions entice us to skip the complexities that may follow. Nonetheless, truths are usually true. There are exceptions to everything and any point can be taken to the extreme and therefore rendered flawed. At the same time, there are some generalizations in life that hold true most of the time, and we can benefit from remembering these and using them as a platform to make choices in life. We can teach these to our children so they can learn, before they turn sixty, that there is value in understanding how things usually work and what decisions typically pay off.

Here are a few truths that we believe. Understanding your truths will help you choose left or right when you face the next fork in your road of life:

- **Joy is usually more fulfilling than fun.**
- **Learning is more elevating than knowledge.**
- **Courage is ultimately safer than fear.**
- **Meaningful is typically a better choice than comfortable.**
- **A challenge is inherently more rewarding than the familiar.**
- **Compassion for others is usually more mature than judging others.**
- **Gray is usually more honest than black and white.**
- **Generosity and giving are often a hedge against taking.**

These are not facts, they are guides for the journey and it is important to remember what we believe to be usually true. Though we or our children may find exceptions to these truths, they still merit being valued because they will usually serve us well. Our children will need these truths when they come to forks in the road, since left or right is not always easy to distinguish.

The GIST of It

- A significant challenge for today's millennial parent is raising kids with a balanced perspective on fun and joy. Most forces in our culture push the "fun agenda" which leaves kids wanting escalating experiences that don't satisfy for long.

- Introducing and exposing our children to joy is important.

- Think about what gives your child joy. Then, try to balance their yearning for fun with experiences that build joy.

- Children will come to forks in the road of life where one path leads to fun and the other leads to joy. Help them turn toward the path of joy. In our culture, this is truly the road less traveled.

- The difference between joy and fun captures just one of many truths that we can remind ourselves of and teach to our children as they grow.

CHAPTER FIVE:
CHECKLIST FOR ADULTHOOD

Imagine what it would be like to have a checklist for adulthood—a list of prerequisites for young people to complete before they would be considered adult. To our knowledge, a list has not been compiled and most likely will never be. But, it is a great thought.

The book *1,000 Places to See Before You Die* lists many places to visit, including Machu Picchu in Peru, the Eiffel Tower, and the Grand Canyon. These are the types of wonderful experiences we often associate with a checklist or a "bucket list." They are lists intended to be peak events that give us unforgettable memories. We make lists like these when we prioritize our lives and our travels.

What might be on a list of things that kids should know about or have experienced before they become adults? Everyone's list would be different, but some things that would probably be included are:

- Spring break in the Caribbean
- Getting the newest smartphone
- Hosting a birthday party

- The "best Christmas ever"
- Planting a tree
- Writing a paper on global warming
- Making varsity
- Having great friends
- Going to camp
- Seeing Europe
- Buying that first car

The list could be endless. Most of us would probably include positive experiences for our children, experiences that would fill them with wonder, thrills, happiness, and pleasant feelings.

In contrast to this list of relatively positive experiences, there is a list of things that most parents would never want their child to endure. In fact, if it were up to parents, items on this list would be avoided as much as possible. Yet this list exists, whether you are aware of it or not.

Some of the things you are trying to help your child avoid are actually experiences he or she needs to have.

Kids need to have a certain number of these not-so-positive experiences in order to mature and gain wisdom and perspective. Without these kinds of experiences children may grow up unprepared for adult life. We see this all the time in our respective practices—young adults whose maturity levels are sluggishly behind their chronological ages, and who have little ability to function as emancipated adults.

This second list is far more important to our children than the first. The experiences on this list are different from the first and perhaps obscure enough so we wouldn't typically think of them. Here is a list of experiences a child should have before he or she becomes an adult:

- Not being invited to a birthday party
- Experiencing the death of a pet
- Breaking something valuable
- Working hard on a paper and still getting a poor grade
- Having a car break down away from home
- Seeing the tree he planted die
- Being told that a class or a camp is full
- Getting detention
- Missing a show because she was helping Grandma
- Having a fender bender
- Being blamed for something he didn't do
- Having an event cancelled because someone else misbehaved
- Being fired from a job
- Not making the varsity team
- Coming in last at something
- Being hit by another kid
- Rejecting something he had been taught
- Deeply regretting saying something she can't take back
- Not being invited when friends are going out
- Being picked last for neighborhood kickball

To some extent, any child who has not experienced the bulk of these or similar events will not be ready to be an adult.

Part of parenting your children well is learning to see events you might otherwise try to avoid or dread in your child's life as *growth-producing* events. The main task for parents is to keep their children safe while preparing them for adulthood. There seems to be a lot of agreement on this goal. The misperception is about how to reach that goal. In many homes, safety is out of balance with preparation. Today, there is more concern about safety, followed by an emphasis on performance, but not nearly enough focus on preparation.

While it could go either way, getting fired from a job is usually a good thing to happen to a teenager, especially if he or she was fired for giving free product to a friend or for not arriving at work on time. When a young boy gets a bad math teacher or has his skateboard stolen, parents don't usually think, *Perfect, that's perfect—it's just what he needed to happen at least once in his childhood.* To illustrate this, let us tell you a little story.

Hank the Fox

Once upon a time, a family was out driving and saw a dead adult female red fox lying in the road. In the weeds nearby they spied a fox kit. This little guy was clearly terrified and did not know whether to run or stay. About six weeks old, he was strong and agile, but without his mother wouldn't be able to survive in the wild.

When they tried to pick him up, he struggled violently, but he was so small that his struggles were of no real consequence. They brought the fox kit home and built a wonderful and comfortable kennel for him. The family named the fox kit Hank and fed him grain-free food from the pet store. He had a dozen toys in his kennel and enjoyed a wonderful life. Soon there was a mutual trust and Hank became a much-loved pet.

Their plan was to raise the fox until he was fully grown. When he was ready to fend for himself, they would release him back into the wild near the spot where he was found.

Hank was a perfect specimen of a red fox. He was ten percent bigger than most wild foxes and his beautiful red coat glistened in the sunshine pouring through the living room window. This was the only sunshine Hank saw, with the exception of brief leashed potty breaks. The family knew he would surely run away if unleashed, and he was in no way ready to survive on his own in the wild.

Soon the family celebrated Hank's fourth birthday. By then they had switched from their two-year plan to a four-year plan for fear that Hank would more likely become prey than be able to find food on his own.

For years the family had told their friends they were raising Hank with the express goal of setting him free. Four years into Hank's life, people were starting to ask why Hank was still lying on the couch and wasn't out in the woods. The family wanted to keep their commitment to release Hank, but knew he had no skills that would allow him to survive in the wild. Strong and beautiful as he was, after six hours in the woods Hank would have been looking for a bag that read "Science Diet."

Hank's family reflected on how they got

into this mess. They soon realized the problem. When they brought Hank home four years earlier, it was with the intent of *protecting* and *preparing* him for life in the wild. Now their report card had come due. It was abundantly clear that they had done the protect part extremely well but had totally failed at preparing Hank for life as a fox.

WHEN SOMETHING BAD IS GOOD

Recently, a parent called saying that his teenage daughter, a fairly scattered and unfocused driver, had just been in a car accident. The crash was severe enough that the old car was totaled. No one was hurt in either car, the car was insured, and the daughter was remorseful. Not only did she feel terrible, she was immediately repentant about not paying better attention to the road.

These parents had some training in the checklist to adulthood way of thinking about their daughter's life experiences. The dad found it remarkable how radically differently he and his wife perceived and processed the entire event than they would have a year earlier. They were able to be calm, objective, pensive, and supportive throughout the whole ordeal. Why? Because, they concluded after numerous talks with their daughter about her driving, that it was likely going to take an accident, or at least a close call, to finally get her attention. As their daughter sat crying on the couch that night, there was no doubt they had her attention. They had checked something off her checklist to adulthood, without irreversible damage. Their daughter had taken a huge step toward driving more responsibly.

**Growth is the unintended benefit
of the things in our life that disappoint us.**

Of course, we would never wish a car accident on anyone. The variables are too risky and unpredictable. Likewise, parents wouldn't wish for a bad coach or math teacher for their son or daughter. It is only after the fact that we can be grateful for the learning that comes from any incident or experience that is not pleasant. It is an irrefutable fact of life that events that we might try to avoid are, in retrospect, the very events that produce important growth in our lives. Especially later in life, we can look back and see that almost all our growth is from something that was difficult or unpleasant.

We must teach our children to see that the things unwished for in their lives play a powerful role in forming their strength, character, and the ability to deal with adversity in constructive ways. Growth is the unintended benefit of the things in our life that disappoint us. It doesn't matter if our children are too young to understand this; it is important that we as parents understand this.

THE BEST TEACHERS

The best teachers for our children are not obedience, modeling, instruction, or habit. Contrary to the credo of the popular parenting culture, we consider these to be "pseudo-teachers." Instead, *experience* in life is the best teacher. Wisdom and maturity are the end result of having experience as a teacher. Experiences that involve failure, disappointment, uncertainty, unfairness, and sacrifice will teach your child the deeper lessons of life.

A four-year-old child can and should be obedient. He can follow instructions, take on a habit, or copy what's modeled to him. But a four-year-old child cannot be mature because a four-year-old has not had enough life experience.

"My Daughter Has Changed!"

A couple came to the counseling office with their daughter for help. As the father described the dilemma, he said, "My daughter has changed so much in just sixty days that I barely recognize her. She does whatever her friends tell her to do. They have talked her into smoking, skipping school, lying, and smoking pot. If they asked her to jump in the river off a high bridge, she would probably do it."

Knowing that it is uncommon for anyone to change that much in sixty days, I asked, "Really? How has she changed?"

He said, "Sixty days ago she was an A student, she was trustworthy, she was a leader in our church's high school group, and she was helpful around the house. Back then she would do anything we asked her to do."

His phrasing caught my ear and piqued my curiosity. I said, "I guess she hasn't changed all that much."

"What do you mean?" asked the father with a surprised look on his face.

"Sixty days ago she was a kid who did what you and other adults asked her to do. Now she is a kid who does what her friends ask her to do," I said. "She isn't thinking for herself or following her own convictions. The only difference is that she has changed who she is listening to."

What's Wrong with Obedience?

Obedience, modeling, instruction, and habit are all useful tools for helping us raise kids, but they are not ideal. Independent thinking and self-discipline are the reasons to celebrate a child's completion of a task. It is our hope that someday a child will go out and chop the ice on the sidewalk—not for reasons of obedience, modeling, instruction, or habit—but for another's safety. Any other reason is a different form of playing "follow the leader."

Obedience looks good, especially when children are being obedient. But, it's just a way to describe a child who is behaving the way the adult wants him to behave. Most of the time, obedience has a *deal* underneath it. The child behaves obediently to avoid the consequences, not because he truly wants to behave that way. An external force requires a child to conform to an expectation.

Obedience is the most overrated *false-teacher*, yet parents love to see it. It has nothing to do with real maturation, and everything to do with acting a certain way in a particular environment. A child who is obedient ninety percent of the time may not be ninety percent mature for his age, but he looks good on the outside to his parents and most people around them. Obedience is a wonderful stopgap or transitional form of learning, but it is not a definitive answer. When the environment changes, or when mom and dad are not around and no one is watching, obedience will likely dissipate. Only what has been internalized will survive.

Granted, obedience is an important skill for every child to learn. We all have people in authority over us and we all (even adults) are called upon at times to do what we're told. The importance of this cannot be overstated. The point, however, is that while obedience is a necessary skill, it does not contribute as much as we think toward maturity.

THE DOWNSIDE OF MODELING

Modeling has been another overemphasized parenting concept for the past thirty years. There are several problems with modeling. First, modeling shows the child exactly what to do and how to do it, but it doesn't let him try something different on his own that might be successful or might be a failure. It is an externally motivated way of conforming to one way of doing something. It's difficult to learn how to solve problems on your own if the only way you've done things in your life is through modeling.

The second problem modeling creates is there is an entire menu of options for the child to utilize to drive her parents crazy when she doesn't do tasks in the way she was modeled. If you model loading the dishwasher or vacuuming or cleaning up after the dog in the backyard and your child does it differently, to you it might look incomplete, insufficient, or lazy. If you use modeling, you will have equity in situations it is unnecessary to have equity in. When your child deviates from the modeled procedure, it may create an unnecessary and avoidable confrontation.

Modeling can be helpful in brief and limited situations. It is fine to model how to fold a shirt or mow the lawn. It can be helpful to model how to drive up an icy hill. After it has been modeled concisely, the best scenario is when your child decides how she wants to do the task. She can decide to do it the way you showed her, or she can figure out her own way to do it.

Parents whose kids have significant problems with maturity and behavior have said to us, "We have modeled a good marriage and a loving family." Our question to them is, "How's modeling working for you?" Our experience is that modeling has very limited value in helping kids grow up.

When Instruction Fails

Instruction for the child isn't a bad thing, but it usually involves the parent too much. It's obvious if instruction has been over-utilized with a particular child. When asked to do anything, the child looks like a deer in the headlights. He is paralyzed because he doesn't know where to start. That's because someone has always started things for him. This learned dependence and reliance on the adult cripples him when he gets to a point of needing to do things independently. Parents who instruct excessively usually go into great detail about what they want their child to do and give a step-by-step way for them to accomplish the task.

Please don't hear us wrong. Instruction for our kids is a *good* thing. It is merely overrated and not as powerful as we might think in the long run.

We should instruct our kids in everything from how to meet an adult, how to care for a pocketknife, to how to apply for their first job. All of this is good and highly recommended. Often instruction is better after asking the kids for their thoughts rather than before. Try asking, "What are you thinking would be a good outfit for you to wear to your job interview?" After hearing your child's idea, then instruction can be of value.

The Habit Trail

We all agree that good habits are better than bad habits. However, no habits are better than good habits. They are more mature. It is a fine thing to say, "Thank you" out of habit, but far better to say, "Thank you" out of gratitude. Habits tend to be automatic, things that become part of us without remembering why we even do them. There are good habits—like brushing your teeth twice a day or locking the car when you go into a store. But, habits that are imposed on the child can quickly lose their impact. Too often parents use habits to force behaviors they feel are valuable. But, the child has nothing internally driving him to do what might be considered proper.

Thinking, self-discipline, and experience are the best teachers. They are the first choice when applicable.

The GIST of It

- Always keep the goal of adulthood in mind. Without this focus, you will lose your way in the turbulent journey of raising children.

- You may overvalue things like bedtime, vegetables, homework, sports, birthdays, music practice, and compliance. In doing this, you may accidentally undervalue lessons in failure, disappointment, forgiveness, resilience, injustice, personal responsibility, and kindness.

- Allowing your child the opportunity to collide with life in wonderful and painful ways will teach him much more than protecting him all the time. This is the easiest and most efficient way to raise your child.

CHAPTER SIX:
THE EAGLE STORY

Two baby eagles hatch in an eagle's nest in southern Ontario in early May. For this first season of life, their home is a five-foot-wide nest, high up in a stable tree. Born needy and vulnerable, they are well protected in this haven. They have no predators except at night when a few nocturnal owls present danger if an adult eagle is not nearby.

In one short season, the young eaglets need to become emancipated young adult birds of prey. There is no time to waste. Within four months, these fledglings will change and have the appearance of an adult eagle, except for the color of the plumage on their heads and tails that will not turn white for a few more years. By early fall, the eaglets are as big as they will ever get. Although strong, they have now entered the time of their youth that is the most dangerous, even more dangerous than when just hatched.

Their vulnerability during this time is great as the young ones do not yet know how to fly. The time for them to leave the nest is coming soon but they lack many skills, particularly the skills associated with flying. To learn this, the young birds will practice flying over the nest. They spread their wings, catch updrafts and downdrafts, and flap their wings, all while hovering safely over the nest. After they have mastered this, they take tiny flights to nearby branches and then return to the nest. The adult eagles stay nearby during this month for good reason: if a young one falls, it has no chance to survive without protection. The fully-grown eagle watches with concern, but is silent.

Eagles relive this story annually. Many young ones do not survive their first year. Many fall from the nest long before they are prepared to fly. Those that can fly may not be able to fend for themselves in the wild. They can't yet hunt by themselves and will become weak and undernourished. Occasionally, there is one that is fairly good at flying, but its ability to navigate has not been developed. In 1987, a juvenile eagle crossed the ocean from North America and landed in Ireland, weak and exhausted. No one knows how many young eagles die after being blown off course in the first year of life.

The eagles that survive that first year are the ones that hone their skills over the nest and near home. It doesn't matter how big or how old they are, it only matters how well they can fly and navigate. The birds that leave the nest before they have proven their prowess almost certainly do not survive. There are plenty of winds and storms close to the nest, and the skills that they have developed hovering over it will save their lives when they are on their own in the wild.

The GIST of It

- Allow your child to experience the ups and downs of life with you around.

- Let her hover; let her be tossed by updrafts and downdrafts. Let her try and fail, over and over again.

- By trying, he will gain just the right amount of prowess to survive away from you.

- When it seems your child will never learn what is needed to live life alone, be patient. Watch with love and concern. Be silent.

PART II

CORE DEVELOPMENT

CHAPTER SEVEN:
THE EASY WAY OUT

The first few weeks of implementing any part of a new parenting approach are going to be tough because kids don't like the rules to change in the middle of the game. If your kids are typical, they have wired the whole system in the house (in some way) to their advantage. Children feel content and satisfied when they know how to play the game, especially if they know how to win the game.

The good news for tired parents is that it will soon become easier. Not immediately, but soon. It's hard to say what percentage of parents feel tired of the arguments, tired of the nagging, tired of the rules, and tired of the silly situations that just keep repeating themselves and never go away. Perhaps most exhausting, they realize they don't know what to do.

Once you understand it, this new parenting approach is much easier than you might imagine, because you will focus on what is important and what works. If it is not important or doesn't work, you don't need to be doing it. Much parenting energy is spent on a failing approach that doesn't work, serves no purpose, or engages in battles that don't need to be fought. Once you learn to see a situation differently, many parenting challenges will go away on their own and without effort.

However, if you misperceive a situation, a simple problem may never go away. Always remember if your premise is wrong, most likely everything you do after that could be wrong.

Laddie

I (Michael) once picked out a puppy at a local Humane Society. I didn't know the story of where Laddie came from, but he was a beautiful dog. He was also absolutely terrified. He trembled constantly for the first few days after my family brought him home. We speculated about what type of terrible abuse he must have suffered earlier in his life. Within a few days, his trembling changed to cowering. I assumed, as frightened as he was, he must have been abused and needed attention and reassurance to heal. I concluded that with his unknown nightmare past he needed to know that he was safe and loved in our home to be able to stop cowering.

Reassuring Laddie did not work and the cowering did not go away. For months he would lower his head, slouch, and even roll over on his back in a submissive posture when anyone came near. We obviously weren't making any progress with the cowering. Whatever we were trying to do to help seemed to be the wrong approach.

One day I was talking with a Welsh woman who raised champion herding dogs. I hadn't called her about this problem, but while she was on the phone, I mentioned Laddie's cowering to see if she had any ideas for me.

Immediately she said, "You are thinking about it backwards. You aren't reassuring your dog at all as you think. You are rewarding his cowering. Just simply walk away with no words or eye contact the second Laddie starts to cower. Leave when he drops his head."

Within three days and with no effort at all, my puppy stopped cowering. It was so easy it was almost embarrassing. I later learned that I had been thinking about this situation wrong and continued to see it wrong for some time. I thought he needed reassurance to stop this behavior (which I was growing tired of quickly). All this reassuring was frustrating, ineffective, and making me weary. My initial premise was faulty. As long as I was thinking about the problem wrong, I was never going to solve the issue. But, when I thought about it the right way, it almost solved itself.

Laddie has never gone back to cowering.

An Easier Approach

One reason parenting is so difficult is that parents are repeatedly trying to fix something that isn't broken. We believe the following principles will make parenting easier than you can imagine.

1. If Kids Are Thriving, Stop Parenting

Life is the best teacher. As long as we don't protect our kids from life, life will show up over and over again just in time to tutor our kids in the lessons they need. Life is by far the best trainer of our children.

When your child is thriving, wear your parenting hat as little as possible. With a thriving child, you may only need to parent a few hours a month. At these times, your child is consumed with growing and with life. Adventure and creativity are abundant and as parents, we have a front row seat. It's an easy and wonderful place to be.

A thriving child is one who:

- Follows the important rules
- Gets along with others to an acceptable extent
- Performs in school at an appropriate level for his abilities
- Is honest and cooperative
- Shows creativity and passion for life
- Demonstrates obedience when obedience is important
- Lives with age-appropriate courage to face new adventures
- Refrains from breaking any laws or acting reckless in any way

If this describes one or more of your children during a specific time in his life, just take it easy. Watch your child with amazement and enjoy him—without needless parenting banter. Needless banter is all the things parents say that are unnecessary. If they had waited a few minutes, the child would have handled it on his own.

When your child is thriving, give him time to remember he forgot to brush his teeth, or time to call grandma when she is sick, or time to clean up a mess he made. Too often, good parents with good kids talk too much, using words that are not good and are unneeded.

It's OK to tell your child: "You are living your life so well right now that I want to just sit back and watch you learn. When I can, I will try to back off so you can continue to grow. If I see something that concerns me in the future, I will step in and intervene when it is needed."

If or when you are in this sweet spot with your child, stop talking down to your child and stop making obvious or insignificant comments. Give her a few minutes and then see if you need to say anything. It is much easier that way. While this season will not last forever, it will last longer if you give your kids space. Kids in this stage just need the smallest of nudging, and that is how they should be handled.

How easy is that?

Someday the thriving will end, the sweet spot will be over, school assignments will be unfinished, and the arguing will resume. After all, your child needs to push back some to do her "growing up work." Then you need to immediately re-involve yourself in the process. But, you and your child will have had a nice break and you will be reminded of how little parenting is needed during a flourishing season. Also, you will be reminded that parenting is not something you need to do every day.

2. Stay Interpersonally Connected and Emotionally Separate

Most parents are not even aware why parenting is difficult for them. When we ask them why it's so hard, they can't articulate the reason. They don't see how emotionally involved they are in the process of raising their child. They see the child's misbehavior or immaturity and don't know how not to take it personally. They are fatigued and don't know where it's coming from.

Parents often take way too much personally. When your son misses the bus, he doesn't miss the bus *at* you. He just misses the bus. When you are parenting, *take nothing personally.* Your child will do what she does and will likely do it for a predictable reason. When parents take something personally on an emotional level, they drastically diminish their competence.

For example, let's say a mother has a fifteen-year-old daughter and it is Mother's Day. On this morning the daughter stays in her room and has no gift, no card, no kind words, and no breakfast in bed for her mom. So what? It doesn't mean anything. We don't know why the daughter acted like this. All we know is that in the fifteenth year of her life when Mother's Day rolled around, this girl was unable or unwilling to celebrate her mom. She may love her mom or she may not that year. It doesn't matter. That is how she feels that day and a Hallmark card is not going to change it.

Some parents subconsciously believe their love will change their children. These parents want their kids to know how much they love them, but they also want them to know how much they have hurt or disappointed them. This approach is a losing proposition. In fact, the more parents take things personally and emotionally, the more power they give their kids. Don Miguel Ruiz, in his book *The Four Agreements* calls it "emotional poison" when we unnecessarily take on comments and behavior in a personal way.

Look, we have a job to do. It is to *teach* our kids to live, not to make them live a certain way. There is a big difference. It is more important than any job in any profession. The stakes are high.

Most adults have learned they are more effective at work if they don't take things personally and don't get emotionally entangled with events at work. We need to take this awareness home. We will perform better as parents if we deal with things in a matter-of-fact way, and without strong emotions (expressed or concealed). If there are muddy boots in the entry or cigarettes under the seat of the car, deal with it using a wise and effective plan, but don't take it personally.

If your son lies to you, it isn't really *you* he lied to. He lied and you were standing in front of him. Your son simply lied because he has not fully learned the importance and value of honesty. If he is going through a lying stage of his life, he will lie to anyone he can, not just you. It doesn't matter who they are. It matters who he is and where he is developmentally. Deal with the lying in some definitive way. Decide what you are going to do and do it. Teach him the importance of honesty. But, don't take it personally or respond emotionally. He is not lying *at* you in a personal way.

When you learn to love and stay involved in your kids' lives without taking their misbehavior personally, your job will feel completely different. It is so much easier that way. When you take things personally, you will feel offended and your reaction will be to defend yourself. This causes needless conflict and you will make something big out of a non-event.

3. Let Life Play Itself Out

The first question parents should ask themselves when faced with a parenting situation is this: "Is this a situation I should do something about or is it one that will take care of itself if I'm patient?" It would be smart to ask yourself this one question a thousand times a year. When the answer to that question is, "It will take care of itself," then you have nothing to do. It doesn't get any easier than *nothing*.

We can't tell you which situations will take care of themselves without knowing your family or your child.

However, we are confident that you will recognize them. If your two kids get into an argument about a common situation, you will know if they have a track record of working things out in twenty minutes. In that case you need not do or say anything. Or you will realize there is a differential of power between your kids and the weaker one may need some help.

That said, here are some situations that typically require no parental involvement:

- Your child gets detention for being rowdy on the bus

- Your son loses his new Atlanta Braves cap

- Your child breaks a neighbor's window by throwing a water balloon

- Your daughter forgets to buy a present for her friend's birthday

- Your daughter left her cheeseburger on the deck and the dog ate it

- Your late teen threw her cell phone in a rage and broke it

- Your ten-year-old won't come in for dinner

- Your eighteen-year-old lost his paycheck

- Your seventeen-year-old hasn't returned a DVD (rented on his debit card) for five days

- Your fifth grader hates his science teacher

- Your four-year-old left his action figure at McDonalds

- Your young soccer player left her spikes out in the rain

In most families and on most days, all you need to do with any of these happenings is nothing. Maybe show a little empathy, but that is it. There is nothing else to do. Don't talk and don't get involved, just watch it play out.

Learning this principle starts with repeatedly asking this crucial question: "Do I really need to do anything here?" This parenting gig is hard enough without creating extra work, especially when the extra effort is invested in a mediocre approach. And, jumping in unnecessarily is a mediocre approach.

JOYFUL PARENTING

Now, let's up the ante. Let's move from easy parenting to joyful parenting. Notice the third example above. The easy thing to do is nothing. The joyful thing to do is wonder how this whole broken window thing is going to play out. What is your daughter going to do? What will she say when she knocks on the neighbors' door to tell them? What will it cost and who will your daughter suggest to fix it? Some of the most joyous situations we have had as parents started with the thought, "Wow, this is going to be interesting!" Taking a few days to let a situation play out and reveling in the anticipation of how it will be handled is a fun way to parent.

Suppose your son desperately wants a new state-of-the-art aluminum bat for his fall baseball league. You figure out with him that he can easily earn the money by simply mowing the lawn each Saturday during the summer. During the summer he repeatedly forgets, procrastinates, or complains, and does not mow the lawn. Perhaps you go ahead and mow it two or three times because it was fun to be outside on a nice day and twice you hired a sibling or neighbor to mow the lawn. In this situation, the easy part is doing nothing. The joyful part is in wondering what your son is going to do. You don't need to talk, remind, or even teach him a lesson. Life will have that part covered. Just watch.

Months later the season is starting, and he realizes he doesn't have the money for the bat. Remember, you're just watching. Then he has a plan, he goes to his older sister and asks her to lend him the money for the bat. She says she will at seven percent interest a month. You say nothing. He agrees and races out to get the bat. Two months later he hasn't made a bat payment and you hear the kids arguing in the next room about the debt.

Better yet, imagine that he is at a tournament and leaves the bat in the dugout and it disappears!

Why would you want to interfere with any aspect of this situation? It is going perfectly. Anything you do to get involved will just contaminate the perfect balance of life playing out before your very eyes. Even if your daughter comes to you and says, "It's been two months and Joe won't pay me!" you still don't need to do anything.

You may simply and unemotionally say, "I'm guessing you knew that was a possibility when you lent him the money."

As time goes on you may find it necessary to get involved. But, don't get involved until you need to and until you have given the situation plenty of time to play itself out.

You might tell small children you will take them to the beach as soon as they change into their swimsuits and pick up their toys. They are excited to go to the beach and quickly change into their suits. But, they haven't picked up one toy. Instead of encouraging or lecturing the kids you think, "Wow, this is going to be interesting." You hold your car keys and your beach bag and sit down and do nothing. Just wait for it to play out. How easy is that? Even if Anna picks up her toys and Emma doesn't, you still don't need to say anything. Even if Anna picks up Emma's toys for her, you still don't need to say anything. Calmly and silently let it play out.

There will be little or no monotony or tedium when you parent this way.

4. Family Time Can Be Overrated

Again and again, when middle-aged adults are asked about their favorite memories from childhood, the memory often starts with, "The times my Dad and I ..." or "The day Mom and I ..." Far less frequently the memory will start with, "When my whole family ..." This is because doing things one-on-one is so important to our development.

One-on-one time can simply make parenting easier. Doing something, anything, one-on-one with your child is effective, enjoyable, and usually easier than loading up the entire family to go somewhere. This is a great strategy for parents to keep in the forefront of their minds. Going to breakfast, Grandma's house, a ball game, or even a vacation is usually fairly easy when it is with just one child. And, it is usually more effective for connecting and building memories.

As a family unit, younger kids often compete for mom or dad's attention. Consciously or subconsciously, kids keep track of which child is getting the most notice. Sometimes kids just accept this, but they often fight back to win the attention battle. They may speak louder and louder in the car or they may spill a drink or tattle or even wander off. Kids can be very creative when they feel their siblings are stealing some of their rightful attention.

Have you had one or more of your kids being peculiarly disobedient at Target, grabbing items off the shelf, wandering away, or pretending to be unaware he was drifting out of an acceptable radius? The culprit may be competition for interest, affirmation, or attention. Often, these same kids would act wonderfully on their own.

A teen may withdraw, wear ear buds, or answer questions with single-syllable answers. It may look like the teen doesn't want attention, but she is usually acting out hurt because she feels misunderstood. She wants attention but has lost track of how to get it in a productive way.

If you have four kids in your family, it will be productive and efficient for you to repeatedly break-up the family activities into pairs. This can't always be done and the family needs to learn to function as a whole, but breaking up into twos (which is not done often enough) can really help the parenting process go easier.

5. High-Maintenance Kids: It's Not OK

It's not acceptable for kids in a family to be high maintenance. A high maintenance kid is one who engages in draining behavior. They are high maintenance because they are *talked to* about draining behaviors but nothing is really done about it. This kind of child's misbehavior falls just short of being disobedient but is exhausting. Parents may find themselves caught trying to manage an annoying situation all the while unable to spot what is really wrong.

In young kids, these behaviors might be interrupting, wiggling while their car seat is being secured, touching fragile items, whining, complaining about being bored, only wearing certain clothes, etc. For older kids it might be a demanding, "I need the car", or changing the TV channel when someone else is watching, or leaving a pizza box in the family room, or just acting distant and annoyed.

Most kids who behave this way continue to behave this way because this issue has not been effectively dealt with. Kids need and deserve adult attention. But, it is unacceptable for them to steal it or get it by pouting, acting in a high-maintenance manner, or shaming their parents. There is a right way and a wrong way to argue about getting permission to go to a friend's house for a sleepover. There is a right way and wrong way to interrupt someone.

Politeness and manners are important for our kids. If your son got in trouble on the bus, it is usually more important that he talked to the bus driver with respect than if he followed some rule about standing while the bus is moving. An interpersonal and social education is as important as anything our kids have before them.

Implementing this principle will not make your life immediately easier as some of the other changes. But, your life will get much easier when your kids learn that being rude or difficult won't pay off for them.

Unfortunately, parents are prone to over-talking, with comments like, "Don't talk to me in that tone of voice," or "Stop touching ..." or "I've told you not to interrupt me while I'm on the phone" or "Don't text while I'm talking to you." These behavior problems cannot be handled verbally. Of course, if they could be handled with words, they wouldn't be problems anymore as these comments have been made so many times.

First, tell your child that he is entitled to your attention, but not all of your attention. He has to get your attention through proper means. Second, and most important, you must make it costly for him when he is rude or inappropriately demanding. This needs to be done in a calm way. It will be unconvincing to your child if you behave rudely or are inappropriately demanding when you are trying to get him to stop his rude and inappropriate behavior.

Soon after this behavior stops paying off for him, he will use a more tolerable approach. When you quietly take the keys, or stop helping with a science project, or turn the car around and drive home, or disable the TV (especially if you aren't angry), it won't be long before your home is a much more pleasant place to live.

Parents can come up with unique explanations for their child's misbehavior. "My child is ... hyperactive ... exceptionally creative ... special ... gifted ... or adopted." They use these explanations as an excuse to accept otherwise unacceptable behavior. Some parents almost carry these excuses as a badge of honor or as a reason to get sympathy from their friends.

A difficult child might call you out to be a more effective parent and might demand you gain a higher level of expertise, but she shouldn't require more energy. Your child takes as much energy as you give her. Often, the most poignant question is not why your first child requires so much more energy to parent than your other kids. The question is why are you giving this child more energy than is needed or helpful? It likely dilutes the energy you have for another child or your spouse or parent or other part of your life.

Whether your child has attention deficit disorder, is adopted or is exceptionally bright, he is going to need to learn how to be polite and not be unreasonably demanding to survive in life. As a parent, you are the person who is most able to help that happen.

Here is a test: think about the amount of time and energy you'd ideally want to give your child to convey your love and involvement. Now ask yourself, has my child found a way to demand more time and energy from me than I intended? Is one of my kids taking a disproportionate share of the parental energy in the home away from his siblings? If he or she has, then you have a high maintenance kid and something needs to be done.

6. Anticipate The Problem and Plan a Strategy

Even though our kids often surprise us, we really do know what they are like. We know how our kids react in certain situations, and tend to be pretty good at predicting what is about to happen. We know which kids are likely to pull in the driveway late, oversleep, leave the kitchen a mess, and which one will fuss in the aisle at the store. We won't usually know which day these things will happen, but we do know what is likely to happen.

A parent might say, "If I leave the house, he will turn the TV on before I'm at the end of the block." From bedtime to road trips to picky eating to renting a movie on Netflix, as parents we often can anticipate what is going to happen. But often little is done preventatively as a result of this valuable insight. This is a lost opportunity for many parents. Instead of just anticipating the problem behavior, parents need to develop a plan of action when they anticipate something is going to go wrong. Parenting is always easier when we have a plan tucked neatly in our hip pocket, just waiting to implement if needed.

Take some moments on a Tuesday night to plan a response to what we anticipate happening on Wednesday, and we'll think better and we won't find the whole dilemma troubling to handle.

A dad was taking his four kids out for a fast food dinner one night. He anticipated there would be extensive arguments about where to eat. He could have just chosen where to go by himself, but that wouldn't have stopped the complaining. No matter which place was picked, the whole meal would carry the background din of two or more kids arguing and complaining about the restaurant choice.

Suspecting this would happen, he developed a plan ahead of time that he could utilize if needed. When the five of them jumped in the car, the dad didn't start the engine. Instead, he turned to the kids and said, "You have seven minutes to agree on a place to go for dinner. In seven minutes I will ask you for your collective decision. If you haven't agreed on a place in seven minutes, we are going to stay home tonight and you can all make yourselves a sandwiches."

"Six minutes and forty seconds, six minutes and fifty seconds, seven minutes," dad calmly counted down. "Well, what is your answer?"

Simultaneously, the answer came back, "Wendy's, KFC, Subway, McDonalds!" Just as dad had anticipated, they couldn't agree on a plan. But this time, dad had not only anticipated the problem, he had come up with a plan to respond to the problem. He simply said, "No problem, you guys are on your own for dinner tonight. We will try this again next week." And he jumped out of the car.

The next week all four kids packed into the car to go to dinner. Again dad told them the seven-minute rule, and listened as the kids tried to come up with a solution among themselves.

It was fascinating. This time, instead of arguing, they started negotiating. One of the middle kids said, "I'll go to Wendy's this week if we can go to

KFC next week." That was quickly agreed to. Within five minutes, the kids had, on their own, developed a fair and equitable rotation of who would decide each week based on birthdays, birth order, and other creative factors. Soon the oldest said, "Dad, we don't need the whole seven minutes. We all agreed on Wendy's for tonight." Off they went with no complaining.

How easy was that? The problem solved itself creatively and the kids learned an important life skill. It all started with dad anticipating a problem and using that insight to develop a strategy. He didn't know for sure he would need the plan, because they might have agreed the first week. But, he knew his kids and guessed that they wouldn't agree and he was right. He likely heard some complaining when he got out of the car that first week, but it was a small price to pay for the privilege of watching the kids come up with their own personal solution while practicing a needed life skill.

Why Parents Get Angry

Besides being easier, having a plan has an amazing ability to decrease parental anger. It doesn't seem like it, but much of parental anger arises from not knowing what to do. Mom may think she is angry because chores didn't get done or dad may believe he's angry because his son broke curfew again, but most of the anger usually comes from not knowing what to do. It feels helpless. It feels tiring. It can feel hopeless, especially if we are trying to discipline while maintaining a close relationship.

This is a bigger problem than you might think. When parents don't have a plan, they try to get their kids to behave using logic, lectures, and love. None of these tactics work. Deep inside, parents know these approaches won't work. But what will work?

Tired parents don't have the energy to look up some creative consequence for everything their kids do wrong. They know something must be done, but what? What the parent wants to say to the child is, "Why couldn't you just do what you are supposed to do? Now I don't know what to do and I don't have the energy to fight you or be creative. I'm so angry you put me in this position!"

Having a plan ready to go will make life easier and drastically reduce anger in the home. In many homes, there are regular outbursts of anger and fights about kids being on an electronic device late at night. In some homes fights occur about this issue several nights a week. Having a plan stops the fights, the discussions, and the anger.

The plan could simply be to have Wi-Fi on a timer that shuts off at 10:05. In a few days the family will accept this new reality and find a way to get things done by that time. Even a mediocre plan is better than no plan. Plans don't all work, but you will find yourself getting better at devising a plan as you become less tired and more creative.

Of all the myriad problems facing parents today in our complex world, fatigue should not be one of the biggest problems, yet it is. Parenting is an important and fun job and we can't do it when we are exhausted. We hope you can see some ways to become more efficient by understanding these principles.

CHAPTER EIGHT:

JUST SHUT UP!

As kids and teenagers listen to their parents, *just shut up* may be the words most frequently circulating in their brains. They hear it in their heads all the time. They might blurt it out with every ounce of contempt they can muster but, usually, they don't. It just remains a pounding thought in the silent recesses of their minds. Over and over again they whisper it to themselves: *Would you just shut up?* They don't say it out loud because saying it could trigger another discussion that would produce twenty more thoughts of "just shut up!" Hence, they remain mute.

Loving parents can talk too much. Conscientious parents can talk too much. Involved parents can talk too much. And absentee parents can talk too much. This is an equal opportunity error. Whether a child thinks *just shut up* or accidentally blurts it out, he is probably wiser than he knows.

Parents who talk too much often destroy their relationships with their children. It does no good to talk too much at your kids. In fact, it makes learning a lesson more difficult than it needs to be and creates shame.

This does not mean that you shouldn't talk to your kids! Talk to your kids all you want. Talk about anything except their mistakes—past, present, and future. When we talk about what they've done wrong, we are talking about their past mistakes. When we use warnings and reminders, we are talking to our kids about their future mistakes.

The Consequences of Talking Too Much

When a parent talks too much it is very difficult to keep what a child did wrong separate from who he is. Shame is the first consequence of a parent talking too much. Shame is the over-correlation between what the child has done and who the child is. There is a big difference between parents identifying a fact versus commenting about who he is.

Coming home late is what the teenage boy did. A mess is the condition of his room. In a shame-based home, when he comes home late or his room is a mess, shame tells him he is irresponsible and a slob. Parents who talk too much tend to make this over-correlation for their child. It is very difficult and takes great skill to be able to talk to your child for more than a minute or two about what he has done wrong without perpetuating shame. Soon the child learns to take on a shame-based existence on his own.

The Speeding Ticket

Picture yourself out driving some night very near your home. There is no traffic, the visibility is clear, and without really thinking about it, you begin to speed. A local policeman clocks you twelve miles an hour over the speed limit and turns on his flashing lights. As you see him in your rearview mirror you glance at your speedometer and see that you have crept up to twelve mph over the speed limit.

At that moment you know it is too late to slow down. You wonder for a brief moment if there is a way to reverse the past one or two minutes and slow down, but realize that can't be done. You can't undo something you have already done. As the officer approaches, you roll down the window hoping you will just get a warning, but know that's unlikely. As you hear the officer's steps approach, your more realistic plan is to get the ticket, get it fast, and get it over with. You can pay the eighty-five dollars and deal with the insurance ramifications later. You're glad it wasn't a serious problem. You just want to hear the damages and move on with your life.

The policeman comes up to the window and says, "I hope you are not in a hurry, because I think we need to sit here and have a good long talk about what you just did and who you've become. I expect some people around here to speed, but I really expected more from you. You live around here and you know there might be kids outside in the dark. You even have kids in this neighborhood. You know I saw you go by two weeks ago about eight miles an hour over the limit and I let it go, hoping you would learn a lesson. But I was wrong about you. You are the type of person who needs a ticket to learn a lesson." On and on it goes. Then he adds, "While I've got you here, I've noticed your dog out in the street unleashed on occasion, and I've observed your garage getting more and more untidy ever since you got involved with that investment club you're in."

Slowly at first, then more rapidly, a rage starts building in you. There are little kids out at night in this neighborhood, but you weren't going to hit a kid—the visibility was perfect. And what did the officer mean when he said, "You are the type of person who needs a ticket?" *How does he know what kind of person I am*? Soon you are thinking about all the burglaries and DUIs that have happened in your municipality in the past year that the officer should be concerning himself with. Your defenses kick in, resentment fills your mind, and the words form in your mind, just the way they did when you were a kid: *Just shut up*!

What just happened in that interchange? Let's break it down. When you first saw the lights in your mirror, your first emotion was regret. You were sorry for the choice you had made. That was followed by the wish and the hope that you might not get what you deserved and that the officer might have grace. That wish lasted only a few seconds. An acceptance and an "owning" of what you had done and a healthy willingness to pay the fee followed. Finally, you had a brief awareness that despite great visibility, a minor distraction could have resulted in a mistake with dire consequences, one much more costly than the expense of a ticket. This was the best possible outcome from a speeding incident: just a speeding ticket, healthy regret, and an adequate wake-up call about paying more attention when you drive.

But, you also got a long lecture from the policeman that boiled your blood. This lecture changed the dynamic of the whole event. What if the officer had simply said, "Hello, did you know you were speeding? You may be a very careful driver, but at twelve over I just can't let it pass this time." What if he handed you the ticket and said, "Have a good evening and please be careful on this road in the future." There! It could have been done in twenty-five seconds with nothing more needing to be said.

The officer's "good long talk" pretty much guaranteed that the outcome was going to go in a different direction. Think about blame alone. At first, in the privacy of your own heart, you blamed yourself in a healthy way. By the time the policeman was done talking, you had reversed that whole process—you were blaming him and defending yourself. Sound familiar? Just about every wonderful and healthy lesson from the speeding ticket dissolved as the officer kept talking. The policeman did what many parents do—he expanded the crime. Soon the topic rolled into dogs and garages. What do dogs and garages have to do with speeding?

Many parents think that talking is part of parenting. Without reflecting on the topic, they believe that if they aren't talking, they aren't parenting. Some parents don't even seem to realize they are talking excessively. They may be in the car, in the kitchen making dinner, or at the grocery store and they just talk. Sometimes it's about mistakes, but it can also be nothing more than white noise filling the air with unnecessary words.

Envision this common scenario. While waiting in an optometrist's lobby, a mother comes in with her two children, about ages five and three. The kids are well behaved except for reaching for a few low-hanging frames on a display. In thirty-five minutes, the mother never stops talking to her children. Ninety-nine percent of what she says is unnecessary and quite destructive. She continuously offers commentary about where they walk or sit, what they say or eat—and two dozen other topics. There are continuous threats, warnings, and even some encouragement from this well-intentioned mom. Yet the majority of what she says to her kids is a message of shame and inadequacy. Most likely, this mother is unaware of the negative impact of her excessive words.

Talking too much is nothing more than white noise, filling the air with unnecessary words.

In Garrison Keillor's classic book, *Lake Wobegon Days*, he writes of Harold, a middle-age man raised in Lake Wobegon, who left town and returned home twenty years later to nail to the door of the Lutheran church his own personal 95 theses. It was a brief manifesto written as a formal complaint against his childhood. It contained the ninety-five things he learned growing up. He likely had a mother similar to the one in the optometrist's office. Harold concludes his document with this summary:

> My posture, facial expression (if any), tone of voice, gait, all were of constant critical interest as you strove to achieve a perfect balance in me.
> "Sit up. Don't slouch."
> Then, "Relax. You make me nervous just to look at you."
> "Why such a gloomy look?" Then, "Wipe that smirk off your face."
> "Pick up your feet." Then, "Can't you walk without sounding like a herd of elephants?"
> "Speak up. Don't mumble." "Keep your voice down."
> Now you call me on the phone to ask, "Why don't you ever call us?"

Harold points out that when he does call his parents, they are mostly disinterested in hearing about his life – they are just hurt that he hasn't called. Harold concludes that he doesn't need to call home anymore because every day he still hears his parents' critical messages in his head. He even leaves the radio on to block out their voices to no avail and assumes that he will hear their voices until the day he dies.

It would be hard to measure the actual percentage of parents who talk too much. For some parents, this is not really an issue. We just know that it is quite common in both of our professional practices to see parents who talk far too much *at their children* when most of what they say is unnecessary, repetitive, and destructive.

It is certainly a great thing to talk to your kids about their dreams, accomplishments, friends, and imagination. But, too much talking about their behavior, including mistakes, failures, corrections, and meaningless comments, serves no purpose except to inflict shame and resentment. You don't need to say something to your child that he or she already knows and you don't need to engage in meaningless banter or parent-talk with your child when you're buckling him in a car seat or he is riding in a grocery cart. It just hurts your relationship with your child.

One night, a twenty-eight-year-old professional woman was sitting in a pub in Chicago with eight of her friends. These were highly educated and successful young adults who were well into their careers. Their conversation morphed into how most of them still hear their parents' critical voices in their heads, sometimes daily. Ten years after leaving home, these voices were still a common occurrence. This dynamic stemmed from parents who talked too much. The consensus was that most of their parents' excessive talking had to do with corrections. On this night, the most frequent echo in their heads was, "Have you done your homework?" It really doesn't matter what the echo was. An adult who has been out of the home for a decade should not still hear a parent's critical voice.

**Say what you need to say,
say it once, and move on.**

Parents should use a chart, a consequence, a nod of the head, a wink, a Post-It note, or any other creative response—anything but incessant talking about chores, corrections, warnings, or failures. Say what you need to say, say it once, and move on. This will help reduce shame in your children.

THE "WHAT HAVE I DONE WRONG?" TRAP

Don't be fooled if your child says, "Mom, tell me what I have done wrong." Be warned: it could be a clever strategy on the part of your child. If your child wants to talk about why she was an hour late coming home or why she saw a different movie than the one agreed upon, she is most likely setting up her defense. If you talk, you're falling into the trap. When she asks, "What have I done wrong?" she really wants to find out:

- How much you know about what happened,
- If you have weakness in your position as a parent,
- If she can blame someone or something else, or
- If she can wear you down. Exhausting a parent is one of a child's greatest strategies. Amen?

Your child may want to talk about what happened to her missing assignments. But, most likely her goal is to argue that it's the teacher's fault, the teacher didn't explain the assignment well enough, or the assignment was done but got lost. The poorest response to this situation is to get caught up in your child's excuses, blaming, or justifications. It would only marginally be better to tell the child to take responsibility for herself and that the situation is her fault. The best (and easiest) response would be to say, "That may be. The teacher might be at fault but you need to get your assignments in. It really doesn't matter to me whose fault it is. Your assignments have got to be turned in."

Exhausting a parent is one of a child's greatest strategies.

Very seldom does a child or teen ever want to talk about something he or she has done with genuine contrition or repentance as the goal. If it does happen, you are fortunate and it will likely be a short conversation. Most of the time kids know exactly what they have done wrong. Don't be fooled.

The GIST of It

- Parents need to change how they think about talking to their kids. Too much talking about behavior— whether good or bad—fosters shame.

- Talk to your child about their dreams and friends and imagination.

- Parenting does not equal talking.

CHAPTER NINE:
SELF-PROTECTION

*We promise according to our hopes, and perform
according to our fears.*

- Dag Hammarskjold

P arents' understanding of how their child uses self-protection will help them parent that child more effectively. Just as importantly, parents' understanding of their own use   of self-protection and how it intersects with their child's strategy will make them a better parent. Usually what we are protecting ourselves from is fear or shame. Shame is the sense of having lost value as a person because of mistakes, failures, or rejection.

We as parents may sense a loss of value as a person when certain things happen to us. We may receive a glare from an angry child, a mumbled profanity, a forgotten birthday, or a poor "report card" from the child. Anything can trigger the belief that we have partially failed as a parent or as a person, which in turn feels like fear. Yet, it's hard to differentiate between fear and shame, because often shame feels like fear. For both children and adults, fear and shame are at the root of self-protection.

I (Michael) have learned about fear from looking at myself. Observing families, parents, and kids has taught me a lot, but I needed to observe no one but myself to understand the role fear plays in life. I can think back to mornings in my life when fear was one of my first emotions in the day. On those particular days, fear laid around me like morning dew, waiting for the sun or the wind to remove the damp.

On those days, my thoughts and my courage awaken slower than my fear. I am not always aware that some form of fear is present since I am prone to call it something other than fear. It may show up as feeling like I'm way behind, or I am inadequate for the challenges of the day. Maybe I feel defensive. Or, it may appear as just asking, "Why is it raining again?" I seldom even think of the role fear plays in my life because I do not care to identify it. I would rather eradicate the feeling before stopping to take its pulse.

Whatever my specific thoughts or behaviors might have been on these days, they undoubtedly fit nicely into the categories of self-protection, busyness, or courage. Courage is the only solution that takes the time to stare at the problem long enough to face it. My experience with fear is not unique. In part, many of us create our own fears through the way we look at the world and the way we see things. If we see something as a threat, we feel fear. Unfortunately, we often use self-protection and busyness to deal with the fears that we carry. When we do this, we don't take the time to look at the way we see the world or the thoughts that generated the fear in the first place. In effect, we try to eliminate the impact of the fear before we unpack it to look at its composition.

When we don't notice the role fear is playing in our lives, we also don't notice when we are self-protecting from the fear. Our goal for dealing with the whole mess is to neatly keep it all in our subconscious. This dynamic is common in families and in adults and kids alike. People try to manage unexamined fears. This, in turn, drives thousands of unexamined behaviors. We see and describe ourselves, and others, by these behaviors.

"He's full of rage!" "She is withdrawn." "I am a perfectionist." "You blame everybody."

Unexamined fears drive thousands of behaviors.

We can parent (and exist together) in healthier ways if we can learn to understand some of these behaviors in the light of what they are: self-protection strategies. These are simply tools we all use to manage a world that can feel too frightening at times. Self-protection drives many of the behaviors that kids engage in that are annoying and ineffective. When a child believes he has failed at something, he senses a loss of value as a person and will usually initiate one or more of the six self-protection strategies.

How Self-Protection Looks

There are six types of self-protection of which we are aware. There may be more, but just about every self-protection strategy fits nicely into one of these six categories. Most people use one or two primary strategies to protect themselves. Most often, these are skills learned in childhood that served their purpose well for a while. All of these strategies work, but each can have a cost in our lives and in our relationships if they are overused. Learning about self-protection will be as helpful for understanding yourself as it is for understanding your child.

First we will talk about the six ways we, and our children, self-protect, and then the cost of each strategy on our relationships. They are all self-protection strategies in and of themselves and are not in any particular order. No strategy is worse or better to have: they are just different.

1. Withdrawal

Withdrawal is the first form of self-protection. It involves protecting the soul by just pulling back. It says, "I want to be alone so don't bother me." This strategy involves a person deciding that sharing their thoughts, emotions, or story is just too dangerous and risky. They keep everything inside and refuse to tell anyone what is going on. The easiest way for them to accomplish this is to escape and check out of everyone else's life.

Kids will use TV, video games, headphones, pot, or just about anything else to help them not be interpersonally present. A teen might spend excessive amounts of time in his room "wired in." No one is going to know what this teen is feeling or thinking. Wearing headphones helps him project the message: "Don't bother me!" Many who use this form of self-protection may not even be aware of it. It becomes their way of functioning.

Adults use this as well. A mom might watch a lot of TV or spend endless hours in the garden. She likely won't argue much or share her opinions with any regularity. A dad who uses withdrawal may work late or spend endless hours under the car, or in the garage, emotionally engaged with a Harley Davidson or his tool collection. Or he may be the dad who has four beers every night and sits with his remote Super-Glued to his index finger.

2. Rage

The second self-protection strategy is rage. Rage usually functions as a way of saying to another person, "Get away from me!" Even more accurately it says, "Get away from my emotions!" Rage is a warning to others: don't bring up that topic again; don't do that behavior again; don't make me feel this way again. Or, it may be saying, "I don't want to feel this fear right now." All of these are subconscious thoughts for rage.

Rage is different from anger, which is more of an inward emotion. Anger is a frequently mislabeled emotion. It usually carries the connotation of frustration. Rage (at least interpersonally) is designed to make someone get away or get back. Rage is essentially a maladaptive way for someone to handle anger.

Children (and adults) who use rage are trying to train those around them to act in a certain manner. Training is a major goal of rage. This is why there is so much rage in alcoholic homes. Family members are trying to train each other.

Let's imagine a parent who walks by the family computer and sees that Facebook is booted up. Out of curiosity, the mom or dad decides to look at a couple of photos. Their teen returns to the room and totally blows up. His rage is designed, in part, to train the parent to never look at his Facebook page again. If a teen uses rage after his parent has just searched his room, the purpose of the rage is not anger that the room was searched. The teen's purpose is to warn the parent they better never ever do that again, otherwise he will "lose it." The teen is training his parents to stay out. This is usually done on a subconscious level of thinking.

Rage is a maladaptive way to handle anger.

In the same way, an older brother might go ballistic when his younger brother picks up the video game controller and starts to play. He yells and screams, throws things, and physically pushes his brother, all the while "training" his little brother to never interrupt one of his video games again.

Those on the receiving end of rage pull away from the person because it isn't safe. The impact on relationships can be significant and entire family systems can end up "walking on eggshells" around the rage-prone family member, whether child or adult. When we see that rage has little to do with anger, we can clearly see that it is really a self-protective strategy to train people around us. In fact, looking at rage this way causes it to lose power to a great extent and can even make it intriguing.

3. Blame

Blame is a form of self-protection that is probably the easiest to understand and describe. Blame simply means that the person self-protects by making whatever his problem is somebody else's fault. Children can be very creative in the excuses they fabricate. At times, this strategy can be downright funny if it weren't so heartbreaking.

A teen may say, "It isn't my fault that my assignment isn't done. Mr. Jones didn't explain it at all in class and when I went to his room during study hall, he wasn't there." Or, "Those aren't my cigarettes ... I'm just keeping them for a friend." Any adversity, problem, or mistake is always somebody else's fault.

The world really doesn't care who's to blame.

Adults use this strategy as well. A dad may say, "I'm sorry I got mad, but when I saw all the mess in this room, I just lost it." The dad is not taking responsibility for getting mad because it's his kid's fault. A mom may say, "It's not my fault I'm late picking you up. I had to go to the grocery store first and the checkout person was pathetically slow." Or, she may say, "Sorry I burned the lasagna ... Grandma called right when I was about to take it out of the oven." All of this is so unnecessary. All a parent needs to say is, "I'm sorry. It's my fault."

Kids who are blamers need their parents to give them this message: "The world really doesn't care who's to blame." Many parents would recoil at the thought of saying such a thing to their child, but blamers need to hear it.

4. Perfectionism

The fourth strategy of self-protection is *doing it perfectly*. This is particularly appealing to people who are already doing life ninety-five percent perfectly. Then the thought strikes them: *I am only five percent away from being perfect.* They could be immune from fault, criticism, or shame if they do it perfectly. With a little extra effort they feel they could handle that five percent and they will be safe. Working at being perfect helps them avoid the pain of life, feeling defective, having a lapse, or overlooking something. It protects them from criticism and avoids fault. They're always thinking of ways to do things more perfectly.

This might be the twelve-year-old girl who is stressed if she doesn't wear the "right" outfit or the skinny teenager who becomes horrified when she jumps on the scale and has gained four pounds. Students may act depressed if they only get a ninety-three percent on their English papers. Perfectionists want their Facebook pictures perfect, their hair perfect, and their car perfect. This may not manifest necessarily in being perfectly neat. They may want it perfectly messy, just as long as it is perfect to them. We see teen perfectionists far less often in therapy than the users of other strategies because they tend to function at a high level.

Kids who strive for perfection tend to be unaware of the Law of Diminishing Returns. They can spend an inordinate amount of extra time on grades, sports, music, or dance to gain little in outcome. Perfectionists work themselves to the bone and burn both ends of the candle. They eventually run out of energy to keep the facade going.

A perfectionist wants others to like her. She becomes very troubled if anyone is angry with her or misunderstands her, even if it's someone who is insignificant in her life. Being perfect to her means, "Nobody dislikes me."

5. Self-Contempt

Self-contempt is another strategy of self-protection. It might be the hardest to describe, but if you know someone who uses it, you will recognize this strategy quickly. The goal of self-contempt is to lower one's own expectations every time he or she is about to fail. The message to those around is, "Don't expect much from me." It essentially is a way to deal with anticipated or impending failure.

Imagine a tenth grader who is asked in August what level of grades she would like to get for the upcoming school year. She answers, "I would like to make the B honor roll." By October, she is asked again about her grades and this time she answers, "I would like to get Cs." By early December when asked a third time, her answer is, "I just want to pass." This teen lowered her expectations month by month to avoid facing the pain of failure. Lowering expectations is the hallmark trait of this strategy. It's not typically an issue of incapability; it's an issue of anticipated failure. Past failures have taken a toll in those who have self-contempt and it becomes a self-fulfilling reality of their daily experience.

Self-contempt is not typically an issue of incapability, but of anticipated failure.

"I just won't get a driver's license" or "I won't drive to the mall anymore because last time I got lost" is how this might sound from a teen. Younger kids might stop skateboarding after a bad fall or quit a sport after not making the "A" team. A child with self-contempt may prefer transferring to the lowest math class rather than working hard on her homework. These children self-protect by expecting less of themselves, and take on the mantra of "Why should I even try?"

Parents may unknowingly collaborate with this agenda. They may start backing off on expectations they have for their son when they see he is obviously demoralized and drowning in the responsibilities before him. This is a misguided effort to try to keep a child feeling good about himself. By doing this, a parent co-signs with this lowering of expectations for their child. A mom or dad will become hesitant or frightened to hold their child to nearly any expectation if they see he is barely coping with the stress of life. There is an understandable and natural instinct in this perception.

One solid strategy that can be used effectively to help an overwhelmed child is to lower expectations to a reasonable level. However, lowering expectations to zero will not help at all. Stressed and overwhelmed kids need the tasks facing them to be pared down at times to increase hope when they feel too dejected. The difficulty here is that a child starts feeling another form of hopelessness when he has no achievements to count as his own. Parents are called upon at times to lighten a load for a child, but over-lightening the load will contribute to self-contempt in the child and won't provide the safety or self-love you hoped to achieve.

As a parent, lowering your expectations for yourself will usually not lead you to a better place with your child, though the desire for a break can be completely understandable. One of the unique traits of parenting is that you can't quit. We have heard frustrated and depleted parents exclaim, "I quit!" Sometimes this is followed by a slight grin as they realize (short of a court hearing) that this is a job where quitting isn't an option. We've seen exasperated parents who can't go on anymore simply decide to take some time off and just let their teenager run wild for a week or two. This usually doesn't produce anything positive for the parent or the child—or give them a break either.

6. Using Power to Protect

Striving for power can look like rage but it is very different. Remember the goal of rage is to communicate, "Get away from me" or "Don't ever do that again." The goal of striving for power is two-fold: to make sure the other person doesn't get too close, but also not too far away. It's a combination of a coexistent force field and magnet between two parties. Striving for power has a very unique energy. The one who strives for power sends constant reminders to the other person of who really has the power. The message is, "You can't confront me because you need me."

Here is an absurd example of this. Imagine that the owner of a company arrives thirty minutes late for a very important meeting, sits down, and makes the following statement, "I know I am late to the meeting and I welcome anyone who wants to confront me on that, but first, I would like to remind you who signs your paycheck."

In our professions, we see this in families where there is emotional abuse. There might be a statement like this, "You can file for divorce if you want, but I will get the best attorney in the county and I'll make sure everyone knows about your drinking and you will never ever see your children again." You can see how this statement conveys, "You cannot get close to me and you also can't get away."

Not every example of power is this obvious. It can just be the control someone has over another. Imagine a home with a single parent mom who has a job that involves working some late evenings. Suppose this mom has an eleven, fourteen, and seventeen-year-old. The mom depends on her seventeen-year-old son to help with the driving for his siblings when she has to work late. The son violates some family rule or acts out in some way. With an arrogant smirk, he looks at his mom and says, "So, why don't you take my car away?" He knows full well that she cannot do that because he is a taxi driver for the younger kids and she needs him.

The Price of Over-Using Self-Protection

Each of these self-protection strategies has its own consequence. Unfortunately, our strategies do more than accomplish what we intend, the avoidance of pain. When any of the strategies are over-utilized, they come with a price to the person and those around them. Whether medically or emotionally, there is always a price to pay for avoiding pain. From oxycodone use, to playing endless hours of video games, to not looking for work, there is always a cost.

1. Withdrawal

People who overuse this strategy will most likely be lonely. They may or may not be aware of it. When someone has used withdrawal since they were young, they are not aware they are lonely. Those around them will recognize this because there will be a lack of closeness in their relationships. Withdrawing to self-protect usually starts for kids in junior high school, but people will adopt this strategy all through life. Men and women in a bad marriage, or a bad job, will keep their thoughts and feelings to themselves. When it is not safe to talk, some people just stay quiet. When it is not safe to stay in a room, some people just leave the room. This is sad to see but it is not complicated. In a teen or adult the result is always that the person leans toward isolation rather than community.

2. Rage

The child who uses rage will become secluded. People around him learn quickly that it's not pleasant to be in his presence and will pull away because the relationship is too unsafe and difficult. It is sad that many children who use rage will find themselves without a mentor in a parent. When a kid uses rage all the time, it essentially results in his parent staying away. This becomes a problem when they do want a parent involved. They can be left to face life on their own.

3. Blame

When a person overuses blame, they just never seem to

grow up. A seventy-year-old blamer will never have grown up. We all grow from our mistakes, but only from the mistakes that we don't blame on others. Think about it this way, if a person blames 2000 of their mistakes on someone else, 2000 growth-producing possibilities have been missed. Ultimately, passing up that many opportunities to grow will slow or stop anyone from maturing. If you have a child who is a blamer, he will gradually fall behind his peers.

4. Perfection

Not being known by others and exhaustion are two costs to those who use perfection as a self-protection strategy. It is not easy trying to do everything right. No one can do everything right, so the perfectionist will invariably be tired. Also, she will have to hide those things she didn't do perfectly, making others perceive her as shallow or elusive. Eventually, it will result in other people feeling as if they don't really know her.

5. Self-Contempt

Kids who use self-contempt to self-protect, will experience a lowering of self-esteem. A child using this strategy has a lower self-esteem today than he had two years previously. Every time he lowers what he expects from himself, he loses respect for himself. Even though he fails less, his self-expectations are diminished. It becomes impossible for him to like or respect who he is.

6. Power

Lack of intimacy in relationships is the cost to those over-using power to protect. They may have lots of acquaintances but few close and meaningful friends. If you're in relationship with someone like this, you will probably feel consistent "come close" and "get away" messages.

GIVE IT A REST

Here's an important tenet for parents to be aware of with self-protection: when a child is actively engaged in his mode of self-protection, all attempts to discipline, talk, and negotiate should be postponed. Kids in high arousal states do not learn or reason or receive guidance well. If your child is in the middle of a rage, do not try to reason with him. It won't work. If your child has withdrawn to her room, don't try to force yourself into her life to "talk about things." It won't work. If your child is going on about what a loser he is, don't try to convince him otherwise until he is out of that state of mind. It just won't work.

Here's a fascinating thought on self-protection. Think about how your child's primary mode(s) of self-protection intersects and interacts with your primary mode of self-protection. Imagine a mom or dad who has brought yelling and screaming into the family system. Put that together with their child who uses self-contempt. You have a problem. The raging parent will contribute greatly to the lowered self-esteem of his child, many times without even realizing it. Put a power-striving child in a home with a withdrawing parent, and see who runs the roost. The parent will feel as if she is steamrolled every day and is living in fear of her child.

In conclusion, everyone uses one or more of these strategies to avoid the pain that comes with life. Life is tough and we need to have some protection from difficult times. All six of these can be used without too many consequences or problems as long as they are rarely used. But, overusing any one of the self-protection strategies without being aware of the price can lead to interpersonal consequences. Those who use all six strategies at different times have an easier time growing up than someone who overuses one or two.

The GIST of It

- Remembering that fear drives behavior and emotion helps us understand each other.

- In our relationships, some of what we call misbehavior or personality is really a form of self-protection.

- There are innumerable ways to self-protect but most of these fit nicely into one of six categories.

- While these six strategies work to protect, each has a predictable and undesirable cost that makes it an ineffective strategy for life.

- The self-protective strategies of family members will interact in unique ways with the differing strategies of other family members.

CHAPTER TEN:
BECAUSE IT WORKS

The parents of a four-year-old girl were asked to come pick up their daughter from daycare. She had been pestering the other kids in the daycare, was aggressive with toys, and basically creating chaos. Few two-income families can afford (financially or emotionally) to have a daycare terminate services for a difficult child. The parents were at a loss as to why and were frantic to find a solution.

In most situations, the reason why a child repeatedly misbehaves is … *because it works*. It's as simple as that. Pouting works, whining works, forgetting works, anger works, hitting works, and arguing works. If some of these things worked for us when we were growing up, it's not surprising they continue to work for our own kids. It doesn't matter if your child is two or twenty-two. Most problem behaviors are done because they work or have worked for years.

Usually a child misbehaves because it works.

Why does two-year-old Joshua whine so much? The answer is because whining works in Joshua's family and life. When a five-year-old "picky eater" says she hates pork chops and broccoli, she usually gets macaroni and cheese. It works for her. A ten-year-old gamer who throws and breaks things when told to get off the video game, doesn't get told to get off anymore. Throwing and breaking things works for him.

It is the same for older kids. Why does a twenty-year-old argue so much? The most likely answer is because arguing works in her life and in their family. Teens learn that if they wear ear buds in the car, mom won't ask if they finished a science project. They learn if they sleep in on Saturday they might not have to clean the garage. Sometimes they have learned that if they make a big mess making a sandwich, mom will make the sandwich for them. Many seventeen-year-olds have learned this well. Arguing can work, being quiet can work, sucking up can work, and—one of the most prevalent— staying up until 3:30 a.m. can work. If you live in the Midwest and your teen is living on Hawaii time, you can be sure that this arrangement won't work for you. But it can work for teens. Sleeping in works to get them out of doing housework, giving them more Internet time, or successfully avoiding relationships in the house. They might even sleep in just so they can wear an outfit to which mom or dad would object.

It makes sense that one of the first strategies of efficient parenting is to make sure that poor choices stop paying off. Sometimes the payoff is easy to spot. A toddler asks for orange juice or a snack by whining. You feel exhausted from her whining, so you pour her a glass of juice or get her crackers. She has once again been reinforced to whine. Even though you know what's happening, you do it anyway, to stop the whining. The payoff for her is getting what she wants by whining.

Other times the payoff is harder to spot. A ten-year-old boy swears at his mom and pulls his little sister's hair. Mom tries to make him apologize to his sister and the boy refuses. Mom yells at the boy and sends him to his room without supper. The boy goes to his room crying and yelling, "I hate you" at his mother all the way up the stairs. The mom might wonder what was her son's payoff for this encounter? Surely there wasn't any, right? The boy is in his room crying with no dinner. The problem stems from the fact that what looks like a disheartening situation to an adult is really a payoff for the child.

Actually the payoffs are significant in this story if you know where to look. There are two likely payoffs in this situation.

First, it is common for ten-year-old boys to feel powerless in their world. They may have no power with their peers, none in the family, and none in the classroom. Even the dog won't obey them. Yet, what an amazing sense of power it would be if he could get his college-educated, forty-year-old mother to cry, yell, or throw something! That would be proof positive he has considerable power in his world, a world that is significantly short on power.

Second, this boy probably finds great comfort in a story that he tells himself. He has carried this story with him for years. It comforts him when he is down and relieves him of responsibility when he is overwhelmed. The story he creates might have something to do with a little sister his parents have always liked better. He is less liked, less noticed, and less tolerated. His sister is the chosen one. He is the black sheep. He orchestrated the whole event to secure his ability to retell his story. Kids (and adults) find great comfort in having a familiar story about their lives. In fact, many people of all ages will choose something familiar over something better if the option presents itself.

This may seem counterintuitive, but much of parenting is counterintuitive. As adults, what we would see as a consequence or bad outcome could actually be a payoff for a child. Negative attention, a power trip, a familiar story, and revenge are just a few of the things that kids can have as their payoff. Some kids just are wired to retaliate if they're wronged. The kid thinks, "You hurt me, now I'm going to hurt you." It's that simple. This is one reason why parental anger is so unproductive.

Understanding the payoff isn't the most important thing. Most of us aren't smart enough to figure that out. If we tried, we might even be guilty of over-diagnosing our child. No, determining the payoff isn't what's important. What's critical is making sure the cost of behaving badly is expensive enough to get the child's attention. Parents can do this without ever understanding the nuances of the payoff.

Let's go back to the story of the ten-year-old boy who pulled his sister's hair and screamed at his mother. What thing or things could be utilized to make his misbehavior too costly to continue? One needs to ask, "What is my child really into?" For some kids, missing dinner and going to bed works. If your kid is like this, you're probably not reading this book. The list could include privileges like TV, outside playtime, video games, bike riding, cell phone, having friends over, Legos, or swimming at the health club. Simply taking away one or more of these for a day or two, combined with not rewarding the behavior, almost guarantees that whatever this boy's payoff is for hair pulling it wouldn't be worth doing again. Most kids change after two or three interventions for a particular behavior.

Unfortunately, many parents focus too much on trying to understand why their child is doing a certain behavior. That's a waste of time and energy for all and will be of no help in parenting. The behavior you don't want to see again needs to receive quick and calm consequences with no negotiation. When this is implemented correctly, your child learns that your *yes means yes* and your *no means no*. Emotions are out of the picture: no arguing, no getting hooked, and no drawn-out negotiations, just a follow through.

Many parents focus too much on *why* their child is doing a certain behavior.

If part of the pay-off for your child is power or revenge, much of this will be mitigated by simply not reacting to the child's behavior. Revenge isn't much fun for a kid if he gets no reaction from the parent. Striving for power feels hollow if mom and dad are unaffected by the behavior.

We believe it's most important to calm down and recognize your child is simply implementing a familiar strategy that has worked for him for years. Greater clarification than that is usually unnecessary. You wouldn't be mad at your dog for sleeping on the couch if the dog doesn't know it's wrong. The couch is a great place to sleep on a cold winter night, especially if sleeping there has always worked in the past. Similarly, we shouldn't get angry with our kids for doing what works. Why would you be angry with your child who comes down an hour after bedtime saying she is scared if this has worked her whole life?

THE INVISIBLE GAME

Bedtime is a nightmare in many homes for this very reason. Kids are geniuses at figuring out how to get a little extra time, attention, food, or mischief out of the last sixty minutes of their day. Parents who are unaware of this strategy are no match for a creative kid who has nothing better to do than to try to get some needs and wants met after "lights out." Some kids are difficult and some kids are easy. Most of the time, a strategy called "the invisible game" will work beautifully to eliminate a child's pattern of excessive bedtime stalling. This is not something that you would use his entire childhood.

Obviously you will want to start by extinguishing the overt and covert pay-offs for your child not going to bed. That is simple enough. The difficulty is in understanding pay-offs. Some things are obvious pay-offs like a drink of water, or a snack, or one more kiss or snuggle. One of the most overlooked rewards for children is eye contact. When you look at your child you are, in a sense, rewarding them. Kids are motivated by fun, power, revenge, and attention, but they are also motivated by *engagement*. When parents make eye contact with their child they engage their child. This is part of your child's plan. Eye contact is the earliest point of contact in human interaction. Usually the no-eye-contact strategy is very difficult to utilize. This is because no eye contact is so unnatural and counter to the parenting voices that echo throughout our culture.

The invisible game is a great way to defuse the *because-it-works* strategies your child may have become an expert in. This bedtime strategy involves the house functioning exactly as though the child had gone to bed, or as though the child were invisible. A half hour before the child's bedtime the parents need to dim the lights in the house as though the household is winding down for the night. Parents need to go through the normal pre-bedtime rituals of brushing teeth, reading a book, tucking under the covers, and a kiss on the forehead.

From this moment on, the child is invisible. If the child calls out for them, they should be ignored. If the child comes out of her bedroom, she should not be seen or looked at. The parents should check their emails, go through some mail, read a magazine or book, and straighten up in the kitchen—all without looking at the child or responding to any question or activity by the child. Don't answer a question and don't be a parent anymore, like asking, "Have you brushed your teeth?"

In some situations the parents can watch TV, in other cases this creates added complications. If the dad is using the "invisible game" strategy and is watching the third quarter of a Monday night football game, watching the game might be a reward for the little guy. If this is the case, dad should simply and quietly turn off the TV without a word. If the child has no interest in football the plan might work perfectly. It is important that all this is done with no emotion, no approval or disapproval being conveyed. It would be acceptable for a parent to say with no eye contact, "I can't talk to you now. You're not supposed to be up."

Here are a couple of tips to increase the likelihood of a good outcome. Quietly disable any foreseeable problem. Take the cords for the video games, turn off the Wi-Fi, or use any other simple and quiet way to disrupt the child's stalling routine. Then, don't talk about it. No threats, reminders, or warnings. With some older kids it can even work to flip the circuit breaker for your child's bedroom. Almost all the time this simple and silent plan will solve the epidemic problem of bedtime. If you lost this round today, don't worry. Just regroup with the added wisdom and try again tomorrow. That would be better than falling into a power struggle or implementing a plan that is half developed.

WHERE'S THE MORAL COMPASS?

Kids function differently than how most parents might assume. There often is not as big a moral component to their decisions or behaviors as we might think. They simply lie if lying has worked in the past for them. Can we really blame them for that? They don't pick up their coats if dropping their coats on the floor has worked for them in the past.

It is easy for parents to partially misperceive certain "unethical" or "dishonest" behaviors in kids. Things like lying, cheating at school, shoplifting, stealing, and other behaviors of that ilk can be misinterpreted if we see them through adult eyes— instead of the eyes of a child. All of these behaviors are troubling and they are all semi-serious. However, they are not catastrophic and do not mean a child is totally void of a "moral compass." Parents do not need to feel devastated or hopeless because their child dabbled in an immoral choice.

An adult who did the same things would have made a decision on some level to trade integrity for these types of corrupt behaviors. For a kid, it is not so much an integrity issue as it is a way of trying out the breaking of a moral code of ethics. It is more likely a reflection for them of peer pressure, feeling trapped, taking a short cut, trying out a wrong behavior or, again, doing something *because it works.*

All of these wrong behaviors are serious enough to be dealt with and dealt with in a strong and decisive way. Kids need to know rapidly that cheating won't pay off. But, as parents, there is no need to overreact, or to emotionally panic. Your child is not sliding down a slippery slope into an abyss that is void of a moral compass. He is just growing up.

A frequent question from parents in the counseling setting is, "How long do I take something away?" Well, it depends on the child's age, their developmental stage, their degree of negative behavior, and their natural receptivity to being disciplined. Whatever decision the parent makes, however, should not be negotiated or discussed. It is what it is. Remember, the sooner you give back the X-Box, the sooner you can take it away again. Sometimes not disclosing the timeframe is a good strategy. That tends to work well with the "negotiator child." Sometimes it works to tell them if they try to argue or negotiate, the time will double. Whatever your decision, stick to it. If a parent is confused about what and how long to take something away for, they should err on the side of *severity* and *brevity*. Do not back down, no matter how obnoxious the tantrum. Do not get hooked into an argument. Be calm and assertive.

In responding to a child's annoying behavior: calm down. Your child is simply implementing a familiar strategy that has worked for years.

Often children have legitimate needs they try to meet with maladaptive strategies. Children need to hear their parents tell them that they are loved. This is normal and healthy. It would be appropriate for a child to say, "Mommy, do you love me?" That would be a healthy way to address that need for reassurance. A maladaptive approach to getting this need met is for the child to say, "You hate me, don't you? Why don't you just admit it?" Most kids don't think about what is unsuitable or dysfunctional for a given situation. They subconsciously simply keep track of what works. If saying, "You hate me, don't you?" works to get an "I love you," or works to get a cookie, attention or shortened time out, a child will undoubtedly use that strategy over and over.

Sammy's Story

An eight-year-old girl named Sammy wore out her mother by repeatedly saying, "You hate me; I know you hate me," every time she was ordered to her room for a time out. Mom, on cue, recited back, "No, I love you very much." Sammy would respond, "No you don't, you're just saying that." This resulted in further reassurances, arguing, and attention. The strategy worked perfectly for Sammy. Reassurances and attention were what she wanted in the first place. Her maladaptive strategy was working flawlessly.

Sammy's mom asked for help with this issue. She was told that the next time Sammy implemented this approach, she was to say, "I am not talking to you right now about whether I love you or whether I don't. Right now you need to go to your room. If you are still wondering about my love for you on Saturday, ask me then and I will gladly talk to you about it." Within five days, all of the "you hate me" comments had ceased. Sammy chose not to talk about her mom's love on Saturday when the topic came up. Mom was blown away with how simple the solution was to a problem that had been going on for four years. Plain and simple, Sammy's maladaptive strategy for her legitimate need had stopped working. She stopped using it in just five days.

This may sound like an insignificant and trivial issue. You may ask, "Why not just reassure Sammy of mom's love each time Sammy feels the need for that?" Actually, there are a lot of reasons not to affirm this strategy, not the least of which is exhaustion. Sammy's mother was exhausted by this whole routine. In addition to fatigue, there were other issues like Sammy's manipulation of her mom. Sammy was pulling her mom's strings and stealing control of the situation. When kids learn maladaptive strategies as children, they can carry that approach with them right into adulthood. Flash forward seventeen years and you can almost hear Sammy talking to her husband, who has just conveyed to her that he needs to go into work for part of a Saturday. Sammy: "I know why you work on Saturdays—you don't love me—it's obvious." It is expected that Sammy would use that approach even as an adult—because it works.

The extent to which it holds true that kids *use what works* is amazing. A deaf couple had two normal hearing children, ages eighteen months and three-and-a-half years old. There were many unique challenges facing this family. Because of the safety concerns in a family with two deaf adults and two small children, social services were contacted and a social worker would stop by on occasion to make sure everything was going smoothly.

Whenever a social worker stopped by the house she would walk into complete silence. Crying, whining, and fussing were not effective to get their parents' attention. The three-and-a-half-year-old could talk perfectly and both children could hear and function as normal children away from home or when visitors were at the house. Both children simply pounded on a table or highchair to get their parents' attention. They had learned that crying or whining didn't work in this house, but that their parents could feel the vibration of the pounding and would look up to meet the children's needs. This is a powerful example of just how adaptive kids are and it captures the extent to which kids will simply use what works.

The GIST of It

- Most of the continued misbehavior we see in kids is done simply *because it works.*

- We can't really blame kids for doing what works. It is just natural and instinctual. Whining, hitting, stealing, getting out of bed, lying, and jumping on the couch can all usually be traced back to that behavior working. It is usually not driven by a moral violation or bad intent.

- Making good choices pay off and bad choices costly is the simplest way to try to alter a child's behavior.

- Adults also often use what works. So, be understanding and gracious in addressing troubling behaviors in your children.

CHAPTER ELEVEN:
CASE STUDY: JENNA

J enna was a very difficult young lady. At fifteen years of age she was filled with rage and shame. Her life had been tough, so it was not surprising that she was angry. Her parents were divorced and she lived with her mother and stepfather. Jenna liked to act tough and talk back, she liked angry music, and she liked her privacy. She showed her anger in violent, destructive ways like slamming doors, stomping, punching walls, and engaging in endless circular arguments, especially with her mother.

It was clear to her parents that she needed to work on managing her temper. It wasn't that she didn't have the right to be angry. Anyone with her history had a right to be angry. But, she really needed to figure out how to express her anger in more acceptable ways.

With our coaching, her parents decided they would take a different approach. On a Friday they had a brief talk with Jenna and told her they were going to start focusing on a couple of things starting Monday morning. One of the things that would be a focus was her anger that often turned into destructive outbursts. Starting Monday, punching walls, kicking chairs, slamming doors, stomping her feet, and slamming books down on the coffee table were all behaviors that were going to result in costing her something. Calmly and lovingly, her parents told her that they were not angry with her. They said they understood it might take her some time to change her patterns of reacting to things that made her angry.

As expected, Jenna wanted to get angry right away. No kid likes the rules changed in the middle of the game. She asked, "What is going to happen if I break something?" Her parents responded that they weren't sure; it would depend on the offense, but she was assured that it wouldn't be too bad. Her parents concluded, "It's just teaching. It isn't something designed to hurt you."

Right on cue, on Monday night Jenna was told that she needed to get off the phone and go to bed since it was a school night. Jenna was a child who wanted what she wanted, and what she wanted that night was to finish her phone call. Predictably, Jenna blew up, swore at her parents, stomped upstairs, and then crossed the line. She walked in her room, punched the walls a few times, and violently slammed the door.

Jenna waited and listened. Was anything going to happen or had her parents forgotten about the new focus? Nothing happened. Nothing was said. Jenna wasn't surprised. She had slammed her door a hundred times before and nothing had ever happened. So, she just figured everything was back to normal— just the way she liked it.

The next morning nothing was said as Jenna got ready for another day in ninth grade. But while she was at school, her stepfather came home from work at noon and took her door off its hinges and moved the door downstairs, behind the furnace. To avoid a power struggle, it's important for parents to implement a "cost" without their child present whenever possible. Nothing was said about it.

At 3:10, Jenna came home from school in a surprisingly good mood. She greeted her mom and headed up to her room as she always did. Thirty seconds later there was a violent explosion as Jenna realized that her door was missing. She started stomping around, yelling down the stairs to her mother that she was an idiot and demanded her door back.

Mom, uncharacteristically, said nothing and simply did not respond. Jenna came down the stairs and demanded, "Where is my door? I want it back right now!"

Mom said nothing.

"What did I do? This family sucks. You said the consequence wouldn't be too bad."

Mom said nothing.

"Fine, I will just wreck the house then. You think you can just take my door and not pay for it?"

Mom said nothing.

"Why won't you talk to me?"

Her mom said, "I will talk to you, but I won't answer your question."

"What is this bull----? My friends think you and dad are psycho."

"I am going to make one comment about your door and one comment only," her mom said.

"What? I suppose this has to do with slamming my door last night?"

"Jenna, I am not mad at you and you will get your door back on Thursday. That is all I am going to say about it."

"Fine, then I will just destroy the whole house!"

"That is your choice." And her mom turned and walked away.

In the next forty-eight hours, Jenna brought up the topic of the door several times and also threatened to make her parents pay for what they had done. Each time, her mom and step-dad just said nothing. Thursday afternoon at 3:10 Jenna got off the bus and went up to her room where her door was hanging, as it always had, on the doorframe.

This family had almost no issues with Jenna damaging the house after that day. After years of fighting her on this issue, it was over in six days.

About two weeks after Jenna got her door back she accidentally, more out of habit than anything, mildly slammed her door. She immediately opened the door and yelled down the stairs, "Sorry, sorry, sorry! I didn't mean to do that!" There were no consequences added. She had learned this lesson.

Chapter Twelve:
The Two Things

D o you ever think of all the things your children need to learn about life, about themselves, and others? Have you wondered why they never seem to learn anything?

You've been good at letting them know all the things they should be doing right or better. "Get good grades. Clean your room. Pick up your coat. Stop playing that video game. Hold your fork right. Have you done your homework? Don't talk like that. Don't wear that outfit. Did you send a thank-you note? Stop eating so much junk food. Get off the phone. Help out a little around the house. Eat some salad. Clean up the stuff you left in the family room—now!"

This could be the soundtrack inside the head of even the best kid. It might sound like this to them even if nothing is being said in the house. If you are thinking these types of things, your kids will know. Biting your tongue won't help. Leaving the room won't help. Watching TV won't help. They just always seem to know what you're thinking.

If you see thirty different things a week that your child could do to improve his life or to grow up, he will know it. For a "bad" or troubled kid this can actually become overwhelming. Now, add these messages onto the messages that may already be in his head about shoplifting, bad friends, lost faith, secrets, drugs, and truancy. Understandably, the burden of all the areas in his life he needs to improve can crush his spirit.

The problem is that parents panic when their child gets behind. A fifteen-year-old boy should not have to be told, "Do your homework." This is the conundrum a parent can feel: *My child is already behind where he should be. I don't want to nag, but how on earth am I going to get him caught up to where he should be if I don't get on him about things?*

This becomes a vicious cycle for many parents and their children. Time goes on. Every month that goes by that your daughter doesn't grow means that she is falling further behind where she needs to be at her age. As a parent, you know she's falling behind. Knowing that she needs to grow even faster in order to catch up adds pressure to your days. Combine that with your awareness that she isn't going to grow very much hanging out with the kids she is currently hanging out with. It is love and concern that motivates this tension. If your daughter is like this, you feel the stress.

WHAT'S NEXT?

What can parents do when they realize that a child has fallen behind in her growth? They should do the exact same thing they would do if their child hadn't fallen behind. At least that part is simple. We believe in a concept that forces parents to identify the *two things* their child or teen most needs to learn next. Every kid always has two things they most need to learn next. It doesn't matter if the child is a four-year-old daughter or seventeen-year-old son. It doesn't matter if this is a kid who is on her way to Harvard or on her way to juvenile detention. Parents need to ask the same question about each child as he or she grows up from toddlers to high school seniors and beyond: "What are two things my child most needs to learn at this time in his life?"

Most parents can put a list together of twenty or thirty specific things they think their child most needs to learn. It's pretty easy to make up the list:

- Turning in assignments on time
- Doing a good job vacuuming
- Going to bed without whining
- Not talking back to the parents
- Coming home on time
- Cutting back on video games
- Staying home two nights a week

And the list goes on. What can be a difficult thing for many parents is to decide on which next *two things* their child needs to learn. And then to remain focused on only those two things until they are resolved.

Sometimes the list is more countercultural. A brother and sister may have the exact opposite goals. For a particular child, parents may need to address the following:

- Be more social
- Don't study so much
- Lighten up
- Be less responsible
- Dress like a slob now and then

These messages would be given less frequently but, for the right kid, these unusual messages could be just as powerful and important as the first list. Just know it's a universal truth that every child has two things they most need to work on next.

A mom who raised her hand in a parenting workshop said, "I can't think of two things my daughter needs to work on. She is an honor student, a leader in her school, an award-winning violinist, a great sister, and a leader in her church's youth group. She is also an outstanding athlete." As she continued on with this impressive resume, she paused. It was a long pause as something occurred to her. She continued softly, "My daughter has never learned to fail at anything."

That's exactly the point. This daughter may need to experience what it is like to miss the varsity cut or get anything but an A. In this way, we are all in the same boat. We all have two things we could learn next.

Pause for a moment and think of each of your kids. Without too much deliberation, think of a couple of things that are uniquely germane to each child's next season of growth. Most parents start with more practical aspects of their child's life, like turning in all math assignments and practicing the cello. Some parents may decide to focus on the more social aspects of their child, like talking nicely to the little sister or calling grandparents each week to say "Hi." It's up to the parent what makes the current list of two things. As much as is realistically possible, these two things are what you will be focused on and working on with your child. For example, you determine that your son is going to work on bedtime and remembering his soccer games and practices. Then one night he hits his sister. Obviously, some things still need to be dealt with. As much as possible though, let the other stuff go.

The Two Things is a powerful concept that speaks to the nature of how humans learn. Working on two things at a time is ultimately the most efficient way to grow. A golfer will learn much more about his golf game by hitting a hundred four irons at the practice range than playing a round of golf. In ninety shots on the golf course a golfer might hit his four iron twice. A baseball pitcher learning to throw a new pitch, like a slider, would be better off going to the practice mound and throwing a slider over and over. Trying to throw all five of his pitches in practice will not help him learn the new pitch.

Tennis players have long known that focusing on the topspin backhand down the line is a great goal. If they work on their whole game they won't learn the backhand as well. The only efficient way to learn any shot is to focus on that shot until you learn it well. It is too unfocused to just "work on your game." In the same way it is too unfocused to just "work on life." If we really want to teach our kids new life skills, social skills, or organizational skills, we will be much more effective parents by focusing on two things at a time.

Working on two things at a time is ultimately the most efficient way to grow.

Once you have focused on a couple of behaviors to work on, the question always seems to emerge, "How do I overlook the things we are not working on? Do I just drop all other expectations for my son?" We don't recommend just saying and doing nothing about problem behaviors that are not being worked on. Over time we have found another approach far more effective. This suggestion may not sound like much, but it is extremely effective. To illustrate we will use a simple example.

Jordan's Two Things

Jordan is fourteen and his behavior has been slipping for the past six months. After a difficult review of his grades and conduct, Jordan's parents determine that he is going to work on two things. He must attend school every day and get caught up on every assignment. Also, he must be exactly where he says he is and come home on time (We consider this list for Jordan *two things*, school and curfew, even though it could be argued that it is actually four things. It's OK to connect two closely related expectations like going to school every day and turning in assignments or curfew and whereabouts consistency. They are each a single expectation).

Jordan is told that if he violates either of these rules he will be completely shut down. This means no cell phone, no texting, no rides, no money, no Internet in his room, no video games, no time with friends, and no TV.

It has always been part of Jordan's daily responsibilities to empty the dishwasher and make his bed. So, with the new rules in place, what happens when Jordan doesn't make his bed or empty the dishwasher?

We recommend this simple and powerful approach. Either parent can simply say to Jordan, "Jordan, I noticed you didn't make your bed or empty the dishwasher today. Those are still your responsibilities, but right now we are adamant about these other two issues. We want you to know how serious we are about your assignments and your curfew, so if you choose not to do your bed or the dishwasher we won't talk about it or give you any added consequence. All of your freedoms right now depend on how you do on those two areas of focus. We're going to solve those first. Maybe next month we will revisit the dishwasher job when we know you are keeping up in school and you are home on time."

A comment like this would take about forty-five seconds to say and that is really all that needs to be said. It may seem like a surprising approach to let two of Jordan's responsibilities slide at this critical time. Well, it surprised us too. What we discovered over time is there are four messages critical to the success of the plan.

- This strategy provides a clever and graceful way to send a warning to Jordan about how serious you are about the two areas of focus. The crucial issues are not going to get lost in the chaos of the home.

- This approach conveys to Jordan that you are pulling for him and that you are aware of the struggle the two things might be for him. A child needs to know that you are *for* him and that you are being reasonable. This will reduce resentment which is a primary reason kids like Jordan fail.

- His parents holding their course on just two issues will eliminate several of Jordan's excuses. He can't very well say that they have asked too much of him when they have pared their expectations down to two things.

- This approach is wonderfully matter-of-fact. The parents aren't angry, nothing is confusing or subjective, and the stakes are high. This non-emotional approach communicates to Jordan that mom and dad are interested in seeing how this all turns out, but they have no emotional investment in the outcome.

Jordan's parents can check on the school website to see if he was in school and how many assignments he is behind. The clock on the microwave tells them what time he is home. We strongly favor not asking a child, "Is all your homework turned in?" or "What time did you get home?" Once you have established that a child is not honest in these areas—stop asking. Just figure it out for yourself.

For Parents in Crisis

If you are thinking, *I wish I were dealing with these issues with my daughter. Are you kidding? Write a thank-you note? Hold your fork right? Clean your room?*

If this sounds familiar, you might be one of the many parents who feel they are losing their kids altogether. The concerns that haunt these parents in the middle of the night are lying, drinking, smoking, using drugs, hooking up, failing school, or perhaps even dealing drugs. They're not thinking, *Will my child be ready for college in the fall*? But, rather, *Will my child be alive in the fall*?

These are the parents whose fear for and anger at their child are only exceeded by the guilt and responsibility they feel in themselves. *How did this happen?* they wonder and *Where did I go wrong?* They look at the family album and see the smiling face of a fourteen-year-old in a soccer team picture or at summer camp, just two-and-a-half years ago. *That seems like an eternity ago.* Now, the local police know their child's name and the thought of mom and dad going to Sanibel Island for five days is ridiculous.

What ever happened to the wonderful child who told the truth, did well in school, and was responsible and respectful? Those were the days when school conferences were a joyful occasion. If this resembles your situation, you are undoubtedly scared, confused, angry, and worn out. You may be thinking: *Where can we get some help? We are so far past getting our child to help shovel the driveway.* You may have even had a thought you never dreamed you'd ever have: *I can't wait until my teen leaves the house for good!*

This chapter actually is also for you. The Two Things concept works as effectively as a place to start in this situation as it does for the more benign issues. There are always two things that are the next two most important things for your child to learn.

Chances are if you have a child who is "running wild," you may end up with a showdown. Unfortunately, it is a showdown you may lose. If your child is on drugs, the first thing to address is the drug use. If your son or daughter is addicted, he or she may need treatment and may not stop until it gets to that point. Telling your child this will be good place to start.

PARENTS HAVE POWER

You may say, "The next two things my son needs is to stop using pot and to get up before 11:00 a.m." If that is true, then that is your focus. Do not focus on almost anything else. Your son may need treatment. He may need a drug test. You may need to call his friends and ask for their help. You may need to call his friends' parents and get them on board. Whatever you do, it will yield a better result if you are focused on two things at a time.

"I can never do it well enough" is a lie kids love to tell themselves. There may be a morsel of truth to this, but usually it is self-deception. They may declare this deception with such conviction that you might be tempted to believe it yourself. Majoring on two things will eliminate this excuse and add a focus that will alter the dynamic of the whole confrontation.

When those two things start to improve, other things will also start to improve. This is a wonderful mystery.

Parents may feel underpowered to confront their child in a meaningful way. Most parents underestimate the amount of leverage they have. We see parents who feel their child has all the power. This might show up when a parent tells the child he is grounded to which the child says, "F--- you!" and walks out the door. How much power would you have if this happened? You can't go out in the yard and tackle your son and put him in his bed. He's too big. But, almost always, parents have more power than they are aware of. They have more leverage than they realize. This influence is more powerful when only two things are being focused on.

When the two things start to improve, other things will also start to improve. This is a wonderful mystery. When working with a child on emptying the dishwasher, she may start turning in her missing math assignments or saving money. When a child starts to turn in her math assignments, she often starts treating her sister better. We suspect that reduced stress is some of the reason for this. The child knows that only a couple things are the focus in her life. There seems to be a new "I can do that" attitude in kids who previously had an "I can never do it well enough" attitude. Perhaps she just feels more successful, and consequently, feels better about herself.

GETTING UP

There's a life skill that should be one of the two things for many older children. It is one of the most pivotal, important, and significant things to work on. We see it all the time in families and it frustrates parents to no end. That issue is the child getting up in the morning for school completely on his own. Nothing we have found will make a more broad, sweeping, positive change in a child.

Sometime between nine and eleven years of age your child should be self-sufficient to start his day. That means he uses his alarm. There are no knocks on his bedroom door, no reminders, and no warnings. It is astounding and alarming how many parents are still waking up their seventeen or eighteen-year-olds. It's very hard for a teenager to feel like an adult when he is treated like a child at the start of the day. Think about it: how could an eighteen-year-old feel like an adult if he has to be awakened in the morning the same way as he was in fourth grade? He would be starting his day in regression.

There may be a war in the beginning. There may be many detentions, profanity, tardiness, missed tests, etc. Recently we heard of a seventeen-year-old girl who wanted a medical doctor to write her a note for school saying that she had a sleep disorder and should not be expected to get to school on time. Kids can be so entertaining.

Somehow, parents must find a nonverbal way to get their child to wake himself up. *Do not wake your teenager in the morning.* Some parents have used four or five alarm clocks, some have used foghorns, and some have purchased high-tech alarms that shoot helicopters across the room that must be found and retrieved to shut off an alarm that is steadily increasing in volume. However you decide to do this, it must be done.

Here are examples from two different families of how a child's behavior might be confronted. Both of their situations started the same way: a short meeting during which the parents told each child the way life had been going was not going to be tolerated starting in a couple of days.

Colin's Story

Colin was a twelve-year-old boy in the sixth grade from a divorced family. In many ways, he was a wonderful kid. In other ways, he was a bit of a monster, especially to his mother. Colin's mom came in for help when she had tried everything she could think of and failed. This mom had read several books on parenting, books on nutrition, and was very invested in being a good mom. It complicated things a little that Colin was going back and forth between his parents' homes.

The main reason mom was not getting very far with Colin was that she was working on too many things at once. Her list was long. She wanted to work on: eating less junk food, vacuuming better, finishing a science project, talking nice to grandma, playing fewer video games, picking better friends, and not talking back to mom, just to mention a few.

The first thing we did was to help mom focus on two things. It wouldn't have mattered too much what we chose. The issues chosen happened to be that Colin would get up in the morning on his own, and that he would discuss issues with his mom and not argue (speak respectfully). It would not matter if Colin complied or agreed, just that he didn't argue. His mother calmly told Colin that she was going to back off on her endless banter about how he should behave, eat, and study. She told him that in three days most of the focus was going to be on these two things. He would simply lose his X-Box, his iPod, and his cell phone if he didn't get up on his own and was late for school, or if he did not stop arguing with mom. There would be no discussion and no anger—it would just happen.

Mom was instructed to take away the X-Box cables when Colin wasn't around. If Colin decided to hide the cables she was to just shut off the circuit breaker that ran power to the television. She would do this all with no anger, no discussion, and no resentment.

Within a few days, there was a great improvement in Colin's behavior. But another problem arose. Colin's mom, after seeing the rapid improvement in the two focus areas, tried to add more things to work on too quickly. It wasn't long before Colin's behavior regressed back to the way it had been.

Some parents will group multiple things into one thing ... like being obedient and helping out around the house and doing well in school, etc. These are not specific behaviors; these are groupings of behaviors and will usually limit your success.

Jason's Story

Jason was a totally-out-of-control high-school junior. After coaching, Jason's parents told him, "Jason, there are so many areas in your life that we would like to see some improvement in: grades, lying, how you treat your brother, how you talk to us, getting up on time, and many others. We have decided that we are going to start with two things that we deem to be the most important at this moment. We want you to stay off drugs and we want you to go to school every day. The other things we mentioned can wait a little while we narrow our focus to these two things.

"Starting Monday, we are going to shut you down if you can't comply with these two basic requests. If you are not at school or you fail a drug test (or refuse to take one), we are going to shut off your cell phone, cancel your Internet, you will no longer have use of the car, and we are going to regularly search your room.

"Because we love you, we can't with a clear conscience, allow you to keep living like this. We are willing to overlook numerous areas where you are falling short to make this clearer and easier for you to turn this around. But, on these two points we are going to be as firm as concrete. No exceptions and no discussion. We won't ask you if you were at school. We will find out on our own, so you don't need to worry about that.

"We just cannot allow you to have a fun junior year of high school while you are functioning this poorly. This is your call. You have three days to think about how you want this to go down. Here are the drug tests we have ordered and we will administer the first one on Monday evening. We hope it goes well for you. We love you very much, but if we don't do something we are facilitating your failure. We are not going to enable your poor choices any longer."

Jason's parents may be in for a knock-down-all-out battle with their son. But, almost always, if this approach is done firmly, quietly, briefly, and with unending resolve—it will work.

The Two Things is one of the most important parenting strategies we know of and is simple, doable, and focused. When kids start mastering life skills, relational skills, and family skills, they (and their parents) start to see progress and maturing. Trying to work on too many things at one time results in failure and frustration for all. Keep it simple: work on the two things that your child needs to learn next, and watch the change happen.

The GIST of It

- One of the most important Two Things for a child of eleven or older is to be able to get himself up in the morning.

- Choose two things that are tangible and attainable. Be sure not to group things together like "being good at home." Pick specific things that you want to work on.

- Keep this focus for about three weeks.

- The Two Things concept works whether your child is ahead, where he should be, or behind.

- Working on too many things at one time invites frustration and failure.

A WORD ABOUT SECRETS

The secret life of adolescents may be the biggest hindrance to their growing into mature young adults. Surprisingly, lies are usually not nearly as destructive as secrets. Though they often go together, it is the secret that impedes growth more than the lie.

A ninth-grade girl, with some encouragement from her friends, started to shoplift cosmetics and jewelry. Obviously, that is not a good activity, but the disruption to the family occurred when the girl's energy was mostly spent on keeping her secret from her parents, not on growing up in normal age-appropriate ways.

To keep it a secret, she couldn't wear much of her "new stuff" because her mom might notice. She had to manage her stories, her purse, her make-up bag, and her receipts, and probably her Facebook account. She had to remember whom she told what to, who knew and who didn't know her secret. She had to have excuses ready in case the secret was revealed. She needed to keep track of what her sister and all her friends knew. Any of her shoplifting colleagues could have blown it for her at any time. With all this to manage, she wasn't going to hang out in the kitchen and chat with her mother or help out around the house. Too many discussions uncover secrets. Therefore, her whole existence had to be managed. That didn't leave much time for her family.

Even the most deceptive kids have a hard time managing a spontaneous conversation when they are hiding something. Consequently, they will wear ear buds, use a harsh voice, avoid the main part of the house, act really tired, or adopt a hundred other strategies to avoid a normal, unguarded discussion.

The secret life of adolescents may be the biggest hindrance to their growing into mature young adults.

If a child is avoiding his family in this way, the parents may be able to guess what the secret might be. Often they will have no clue, as it could be anything. It might be a new girlfriend or boyfriend or shoplifting. He may be failing a couple of classes or being deceptive about his outings. This behavior doesn't mean he is hiding something, or that what he is hiding is serious. It is just a construct to help us interpret this new avoidant behavior.

If you sense a secret, it never hurts to say, "I feel there might be something going on in your life you haven't told me about." Notice that this is a statement and not a question. Questions are not helpful in this situation. Your son will not tell you something until he is ready. If he wants to tell you, he will bring it up in the following day or two.

CHAPTER THIRTEEN:
CASE STUDY: KYLE

K yle was a difficult kid, probably in the top five percent of difficulty. As a rowdy seven-year-old he was becoming more of a handful every day. The short list of things he needed to change included: arguing, name calling, not cleaning up his room, leaving a trail of garbage and toys everywhere he went in the house, talking in class (which led to numerous complaints from school), picky eating, fighting with his brother, riding his bike without a helmet, and refusing to go to bed at night.

Kyle's parents were exhausted, at a loss of what to do, and very discouraged when they first came in for help. It was hard to know where to start since the parents were so ready to quit (whatever that means when your child is seven). Kyle had been such a handful and his parents were so worn out that they couldn't stand the idea of trying one more thing that might not work. They assumed that, even under the best scenario, it would take years for his overall behavior to show even a little improvement.

When his parents agreed to give it a shot, the first step was for them to get quiet in their parenting. This couple was far too verbal and it often led to yelling matches. Then they were asked to pick which two things they would like to focus on. They were assured that it didn't really matter which two things they chose. They chose the two target behaviors of fighting with his brother and wearing a helmet when he rode his bike.

Because Kyle's parents were at the end of their proverbial rope, the first evening was scripted out for them more than we would normally have done. They were instructed to have a brief meeting with Kyle to inform him that most of the focus on him would be around him wearing his helmet when he rode his bike and treating his brother better. They were to tell Kyle if he chose to misbehave at school they were going to let the school handle those issues for the time being. At home, they were only going to focus on his bike helmet and the way he treated his brother.

Tuesday night the parents called Kyle into the family room. The meeting started with Dad saying, "Kyle, we have talked to you a lot about wearing your helmet when you ride your bike. Tonight is the last time we will ever talk about it. Starting tomorrow, you will lose your bike privileges every time you ride without a helmet. No arguments and no excuses. In addition, you are going to lose TV, video game, and computer time whenever you are mean to your brother. We aren't going to warn you anymore and we aren't going to discuss these topics with you anymore."

Few things in life were as predictable as Kyle. Wednesday, after school, Kyle came in the house, grabbed a snack, and went out to ride his bike. As expected, Kyle rode his bike helmet-less. Everyone knew this would happen, but this time his parents were prepared. They had screwed a large lag eyebolt into the garage ceiling and bought a cable lock.

This also required getting mom to a mindset where she

would be willing to wait and to wait quietly. Up to now, Kyle's mom had taken it personally when he rode without his helmet. It was all she could do to sit in the house and watch Kyle flaunt his independence in front of her on that first day. Every fiber of her being wanted to yell at him like she had always done and run out to force him to stop riding. In the past, she used false warnings and idle threats. This is what Kyle expected on this Wednesday in late April. To Kyle's surprise, mom did not get angry, did not warn him, and did not even say a word. She didn't even go outside. She just waited.

For ninety minutes Kyle rode his bike up and down the street and around in his driveway without his helmet. Finally, he stopped to go to the bathroom. As soon as mom heard the upstairs bathroom door close, she jumped into action, ran to the front yard, and wheeled Kyle's bike into the garage. She hoisted his bike on her shoulder, took a few steps up the ladder and locked Kyle's bike to the eyebolt (To avoid a power struggle, it was important for the bike to be locked away and unlocked without Kyle present). She got down the ladder and was back inside before Kyle finished upstairs and returned to the front driveway.

Not seeing his bike, Kyle started looking around. He soon found it hanging from the garage ceiling. Immediately he tried to engage mom in an argument, but she wouldn't talk. She simply told him twice, "Dad and I told you last night that we will not talk anymore about this helmet issue. You can try again on Friday." Kyle cried and went upstairs and started destroying his bedroom. Mom did nothing. He came down in about forty minutes and was quite civil the rest of the evening.

Kyle got his bike back on Friday, though he never saw it being unlocked. Within an hour he was riding it without his helmet again. Again, his mother waited for her chance. This time Kyle wouldn't leave his bike to go to the bathroom. Eventually, one of the neighbor boys came over to play video games. As soon as the opportunity presented itself, she locked the bike to the garage ceiling again. This time, Kyle wouldn't see his bike until Tuesday.

That was the last time Kyle ever rode his bike without a bike helmet.

A similar plan was set up with Kyle anytime he fought with his brother. He would lose his screen and video game time for two days and no words were to be spoken. Two times that week Kyle was mean to his little brother and each time he lost screen time for two days. Within a week both these target behaviors had dramatically improved.

At the beginning of the week, Kyle's parents had no confidence that this simple plan would work with Kyle. He was too difficult and they had already tried dozens of ideas. One week later, Kyle had lost both his bike and video game privileges twice. By the sixth day he had started wearing his helmet and by the seventh day he was treating his brother better. Kyle's parents were amazed that he had also become much less messy in that week, he had started to eat a wider variety of foods, and his overall attitude at home and at school had improved without them ever working on the other things or even mentioning them.

Chapter Fourteen:
Tell the Truth

What is the truth about your child... the real truth? What is the truth about how outgoing or popular he or she is? What are his real chances of making it in the NBA or her chances of singing on Broadway?

It can be tempting to tell children or teens anything that will help manage a current situation. We want to lift their spirits when they're sad or give them hope when they're discouraged. Often this includes some type of compliment, encouragement, or exaggeration. Parents may say things like:

"You played great!"

"Everyone likes you."

"Your picture is beautiful."

"Daddy isn't mad."

"Our divorce won't change the holidays."

These words are said to make the moment better. It's not clear whether these untruths are for the child's benefit or to help the parents with guilt or an illusion they carry with them. While this type of comment can be helpful to manage the situation in front of you, there is a high price you and your child will pay for handling it that way.

How could there be a price for words of kindness and encouragement even if they are not true? Could words like that really hurt someone? Wouldn't everyone like a little encouragement?

Comments like these can have a cumulative and devastatingly negative effect on children. Try to imagine a kind grandmother who offers her chubby grandson a double chocolate brownie to erase his discouragement about being overweight. The child may be down because he's not doing well on a diet or is too overweight to play sports. When grandma says, "Here, have a brownie. That's better now, isn't it?" it may sound and feel good, but it's doing harm.

Look at it from another perspective. The real questions are these: How can it ever help a child to see a situation differently from how it really exists? Could promoting a distorted view of the world and of him ever benefit him? How could it ever help him to lose trust in what his own radar tells him or in the feedback of a loved and credible adult?

A crucial, yet often overlooked, aspect of maturing kids (and adults for that matter) is for them to see themselves as they truly are, and to see the world as it truly is. This is a fundamental feature in any treatment or counseling. In fact, the core problem in mental illness is not seeing oneself and the world as they are. Whether the problem is grandiosity, narcissism, or a paralyzing fear—at its core there is an inability to see self and the world as they are.

How can it ever help a child to see a situation differently from how it really exists?

Encouragement is a beautiful sounding word, but if it isn't precisely true it is short-lived. At best, it serves to temporarily alter a situation in order to ease the pain of normal or real life.

No matter how many untruthful statements are said to kids for encouragement, untrue encouragement provides nothing more than false hope. To genuinely help your child with his feelings, the feelings discussion must always follow truth. Trying to manage a child's feelings apart from the truth will be counterproductive.

Distorting the truth to make kids feel better has a negative counterpart. It can be just as tempting to distort the truth in a negative way for the purpose of discouragement. A parent might use this type of statement to shame or guilt the child in order to manipulate a situation or change his behavior, "If you go to school without showering, you will smell and no one will like you." Though less common in the world of conscientious parents, these untruthful statements will also delay the child's skill to accurately read a situation. Loving and accurate encouragement is great, but the power is in the loving and accurate part, not in the encouragement.

A teenage daughter mopes around, depressed, because she was not chosen for a part in a high school play. She might mutter, "I suck at everything! I may as well just quit trying because the director will always pick somebody else instead of me." The main thing for parents to do in this situation is to simply say the truth. What the truth is will depend on your child and the situation she is in and that will be up to the parent to decipher. The most important thing is to accurately and lovingly say the truth with honesty and candor.

Naturally, parents must know how to see life as it is to tell their child the truth about seeing life as it is. This is one of the worthy challenges of being a parent.

What to Do

Let's start with the basics. On its most rudimentary level,

if your son is a slow runner, don't tell him he is a fast runner. If your daughter missed half the spelling words, don't tell her she's really a good speller. If your daughter just had a terrible softball game, don't tell her she played great. Instead, tell her that this was not one of her good games. Or, if it is the case, tell her that softball is not one of her strengths. Be accurate and say it lovingly. What we say to our children needs to match the reality of the situation.

Telling the truth goes far beyond this. The next level of honesty is to tell your child what strength or weakness you see in him or her. It might sound like this: "Dillon, let me tell you what I am seeing in you. I checked your grades online today and it seems you are doing well on all your assignments and they all seem to be turned in on time. Your test scores are not as good, though. Is that how you see yourself doing this semester?" Or, "You seem to be popular at school, but this year it seems you don't like your teacher as much as last year. How do you see this year is going?" Or, "At church you seem less confident with your friends. That is just how I see it. How do you see your time at church?"

It's important to say things like:

- "You are one of the twenty best basketball players in your grade."
- "You are drawing pretty well for your age."
- "Fourth chair clarinet seems pretty accurate for your playing ability right now."
- "You are very nice to your friends but you don't act nice to your brother."
- "Yes, your sister is better than you at playing the piano."
- "No one's that special."
- "You're a little overweight."

These statements are not going to hurt your child. In fact, they are going to give your child a position of solid footing to face a world that is real. Wisdom can only come from seeing the world as it is and seeing ourselves as we are. You may receive some flak for handling your kids this way, especially from people who still believe they can affirm a child into happiness and success. Don't worry about them, because your kids will be better off when they know who they are. Just tell them the truth as lovingly as possible.

Trying to manage someone else's emotions by changing their reality is not kind at all. It really amounts to codependency. It is often true that we want our children to feel better. But we also know that if they feel better, we will feel better, and we want to stop feeling bad ourselves.

We also recommend that you tell the truth about yourself and your own motivations and opinions. Tell your teen that you're going to try to manipulate them into trying out for a school play. Yes, that is right! Tell them your agenda. Tell your child you weren't listening ... if you weren't. Tell your son you don't know yet if you like his new friend Jeff. It drives kids crazy when their parents won't simply admit what they are thinking or doing.

Growing up is scary. Deep inside almost all kids are scared about growing up even if it appears as if they are not. Even kids who have a brash or cocky style may be scared they won't be ready for adulthood when that time comes. Knowing they have someone older and wiser in their life who will shoot straight with them makes growing up a lot less frightening. All children need someone who loves them enough to tell them the truth, not someone who loves them in a way that protects them from the truth.

This relates to why love must evolve and change as time goes by. As a child gets older, it can be frightening to realize he can't trust his own radar or read a situation accurately. As he transitions into adulthood, this missing life skill creates anxiety, confusion, and can lead to unfortunate situations like following the wrong career path, passing on opportunities, or ending important relationships. Life becomes an intimidating experience if you cannot accurately assess your life or know "the person in the mirror." It is hard enough to get fired from a job; it is worse to not be able to understand why you were fired. Without a developed skill of self-truth, life is unpredictable and difficult to navigate.

All children need someone who loves them enough to tell them the truth, not protect them from the truth.

Over the long term, the failure to be honest with your child about who he or she is will result in the child growing into an adult who is either delusional or fearful. Many young people believe the accolades they have been given and create for themselves a world that doesn't exist. A perfect example of this is the hit TV show, "American Idol." In the first few weeks of each season, the show is full of delusional contestants who have been fraudulently affirmed their whole lives. Their false reality becomes embarrassing for them when real life collides with their fictitious world.

There are a few exceptions to this rule. First, if you don't like your child or you like one child less than another, you should *not* say that. This kind of honesty would be far too damaging. Second, do not tell your child how much they hurt you or hurt your feelings. This is usually passive-aggression and can also give the child a way to have power over you. It's like handing them the arrows in your quiver when they have the bow. Just tell them what you didn't like.

THE RATIONALE FOR TELLING THE TRUTH

In the 1980s, experts proclaimed that affirmations were going to be the saving strategy for solving many of the problems that young people faced. The remnant of this thinking is evident even today in schools and pre-schools and homes across America. This was either a very poor hypothesis or one that was implemented beyond its intent. It doesn't help children to be given exaggerated affirmations and untrue declarations about themselves. Telling kids things that aren't true will not help them long term. Avoid comments like these to children over five years old:

- "You are a gifted actress."
- "You are exceptionally intelligent."
- "You're the best pitcher ever."
- "You can be anything you want to be."

None of these affirmations are helpful for a child's development unless they are actually true. As professionals, we are seeing an epidemic of "giftedness" in our society. Sixty percent of kids can't belong in the top one percent.

A man who played football in high school tells about the day he stopped trusting his dad, at least with respect to football. He had a terrible game. He knew he had played poorly and he knew why he had played poorly. When he saw his dad after the game, his dad said, "Great game, son!" This teen knew he hadn't played well, therefore, he knew at that moment he could not trust his dad's assessment of him again when it came to playing football. That was too high a price to pay for an affirmation. It's significant that this teen knew he hadn't played well.

Recently, we spoke to a well-known sports psychologist who affirmed this. He marveled at how many kids he works with who do not know or are not sure how good they really are at their featured sport. Sometimes they believe they are worse than they are, but most often these kids see themselves as much better than they really are. This can have significant impact on the choices a child makes in sports and life. With each decade, more children have become less able to even know how they perform.

When exceptional becomes expected, normal becomes defective.

It is sad when an elite, all-American athlete or superstar does a public service announcement telling kids that they can be anything they want to be. We wish another Division I athlete would do a PSA saying, "I thought I was a big-time athlete so I went to a big-time school to play ball. I wasn't really as good as I thought. As a result, I never played one minute of varsity in my entire college career. No matter how hard I worked or how low I got my body fat, I was never going to play at the university I chose. I wish I had had a more accurate view of myself. I probably could have started for two or three years in a good Division III program."

A fourth grader was asked recently what he wanted to be when he grows up. This boy was an average student, not an exceptional one. He answered, "I'm going to play a few years in the NBA, retire early and become an air force fighter pilot landing planes on aircraft carriers, and then retire from that and serve two terms as president of the United States." He said that his parents and his teachers thought this was a great plan. When asked why he thought he could do all these things, he replied, "Because I'm the third fastest kid in my class!"

The adults in his life think they are giving him a benefit by not telling him the truth, but the cost of this thinking is too high. There is a difference between adults who support realistic dreams a child might have and adults who cultivate unrealistic life plans for a child.

PROBABILITY AND THE JOY OF BEING AVERAGE

Many parents love to dream big things for their children. It seems no one wants her child to be average. The truth is: most kids are average. The distribution of many human characteristics follows a predictable, normal bell curve. For example, height, weight, and length of life follow a normal bell-shaped curve of distribution. The measure of certain mental characteristics also assumes the same kind of distribution. Intelligence measures are a typical example: the average intelligence quotient (IQ) of a population is one hundred points with a standard deviation of fifteen points. We use these statistics to point out that the vast majority of kids are normal (which is to say they are within two standard deviations from the mean). Yet today, it seems almost socially taboo to say this about a child.

It is fine to be average. In fact, nothing is wrong with being average. It's OK to not get the lead in the play. Maybe the person who was given the part is a better actress and singer than you are. It's fine to play on the JV basketball team as a senior when the varsity starts underclassmen. Maybe you're an average basketball player and not good enough to play varsity. That's OK and it's not the end of the world. If six kids are trying out for quarterback, the truth is five will not be the starting quarterback. Part of life is just probability. Part of life is talent and ability. Part of life is timing. A big part of life is to know what's true and what isn't. Parents have a role to play in that process.

We live in a culture that is, for the most part, probability ignorant. The failure to accept, understand, and process probability results in a breakdown in seeing the world properly. We seem to be passing on this probability unawareness to the next generation. If we truly understood likelihood and chance, we wouldn't talk like we do, and we wouldn't live like we do.

If a thousand qualified applicants apply for something with three hundred openings, that means that seven hundred people are not going to be accepted from that group. It does not mean that, "It wasn't meant to be," or "Everything happens for a reason." It means that chance played a huge role in the selection of the three hundred people.

The chances of winning the Powerball are about one in 175 million. People cannot even imagine the probability of that. Our minds are tapped out trying to imagine odds of one in 10,000. Any more than that is "funny numbers" in the sense that we cannot even grasp lesser odds than that. It adds to our distortions when we see Lotto winners in the news every month or two. It is distorted even more if we once drove by the convenience store where the winning Lotto ticket was sold. It makes us think that maybe we were close to winning.

Why write about probability in a parenting book? The answer is because we cannot understand life without an accurate understanding of probability. A teen needs to understand why a friend died in a car accident, why he or she didn't get into the University of Michigan, or why Grandma has Alzheimer's. Without some awareness of probability we may end up thinking that these people brought on the circumstances of their lives, when they didn't. Or, we may think they didn't bring on the circumstances when they had everything to do with them.

Perhaps the teen's friend died in a car accident because he was going eighty-five miles per hour around a tight curve in the road. Therefore, the friend was totally responsible for his own death, tragic as it was. Another person may have been hit by a drunk driver and totally not responsible for his death. This same teen may have been totally qualified to get into the University of Michigan and didn't simply because there were too many freshmen applicants.

Kids must know and understand that a lot of life is managing probabilities.

- What are the odds of getting in trouble if I hang with this group versus that group?

- What are the odds of passing a driver's test if I study versus if I don't study?

- What are the odds of my boyfriend cheating on me if he has been drinking versus if he hasn't been drinking?

- What are the odds of breaking a leg if I snowboard down this mountain versus that mountain?

- What are the odds of a camping disaster if we are sober and the trip is well planned versus if we are stoned and have no plan?

The goal of life is not just to live safely, the goal is to live life alive and take risks in life. How can kids know what risks to take without a respect for probability? This needs to be developed over time.

There is a far greater chance you could be hit by a drunk driver late at night on New Year's Eve than driving home today. Managing that risk is part of seeing life the way it is. That doesn't mean you should go out or stay home, it just means that you have an idea of the risk involved. In rationalizing risky behavior, kids will just say something like, "We did the same thing last year and no one got hurt." When our kids understand probability they will understand that this statement means nothing since an aspect of risk and reward is random and unpredictable. They also will know that other aspects of risk and reward are manageable and alterable.

If you think about teen tragedies, you may think of drowning, rape, fatal car accidents, or suicide. The chance of any of these happening is far greater if there is alcohol or drugs at the scene. Therefore sobriety is a large part of risk management for your child.

Tell the truth to your children. Tell it accurately and lovingly and make sure that you include the truth about probability. You will have wiser and safer kids if they have been prepared to see the world and themselves as they are.

The GIST of It

- Kids need to grow up with accurate and intact radar about themselves and others. Without this trait, a child will probably live with unnecessary fear and self-doubt.

- Inaccurate feedback can be either too positive or too negative.

- Repeated, untruthful, and exaggerated feedback will block accurate self-understanding from developing. It may seem supportive to overstate a compliment or encouragement to make a child feel better. This will have a short-term effect on lifting his spirits but will contribute to inaccurate self-assessment. That is too high a price for such a short-term gain.

- If truthful feedback is done lovingly, it will not hurt your child. Remember that most kids are normal in most ways. Truthful feedback will help kids accept the areas of life in which they are not exceptional—kids need to know they are wonderful, but not exceptional.

- Feeling a need to be exceptional is very stressful on kids. This can contribute to kids giving up on life when they actually aren't doing that poorly.

- Not as many kids as we think are truly exceptional. Our country is paying a high price for this arrogance.

- An understanding of probability and the likelihood of something happening is part of speaking honestly to your kids. Some chances can be highly affected by choices we make and some exist outside the realm of our influence.

PART II—CORE DEVELOPMENT

CHAPTER FIFTEEN:
THE ORIGINS OF SELF-ESTEEM

Webster's Dictionary defines esteem as "to value highly, have great regard for, to respect." So, self-esteem is your ability to esteem yourself. It's your own ability to highly value yourself, to have great regard for yourself, to prize yourself, and to respect yourself. Self-esteem is your journey toward liking who you are.

It cannot come from others; it must ultimately come from one's self. If a teenage girl only likes herself when she is popular and others like her that is *others' esteem* not self-esteem. The esteem of others may feel like self-esteem but it is not rooted inside the person. Celebrities and athletes may have millions of people cheering for them, and yet feel inadequate when the cheering stops. The problem is that these people do not like themselves.

The topic of self-esteem is about as important as anything in life, and certainly one of the most important topics in this book. Given its importance, how does a person lay a foundation in his life worthy of building self-esteem?

Some theories on how to build self-esteem are distorted or unproven. They couldn't be farther from the truth, but have over the years taken on a life of their own.

Do compliments and affirmations from others build self-esteem? Does it come from accomplishments? Does it come from a combination of other people's esteem for us, and how we perform? If enough people think I am great and I perform well enough, then will I like myself and have high self-esteem?

We call the perception that self-esteem comes from these things the Great Myth. Like every other myth, there is a little truth in it.

EXCEPTIONALLY WRONG THINKING

Worse than not knowing where self-esteem comes from is thinking we know and being wrong. Many parents believe if their child feels exceptional, she will like herself. Yet we often see insecurity and self-hatred in exceptional people. Pop stars, athletes, geniuses, all frequently struggle with even basic self-love. So, it can't come from feeling that one is better or more gifted than others.

Being esteemed by others can be addictive for children and young adults. When they achieve it regularly, any dislike they have for themselves is temporarily anesthetized. In truth, performing for others and hearing their affirmations can take away the pain of not being satisfied with oneself. Nevertheless, the core problem of not being pleased with oneself is still there. It is a Band-Aid for a cut and a Tylenol for the headache. Being esteemed/accepted/valued by others is really others-esteem, not self-esteem. The esteem of others never leads to self-esteem it just temporarily helps people feel better.

How many of our children actually value themselves highly? Do they have great regard for themselves? Or, are they just tuned into the accolades that go along with high functioning and high performance levels? Often, children who are popular, good-looking, smart, and involved in good activities have no ability to see themselves apart from what everyone tells them. Their heads are filled with hundreds of compliments and affirmations, yet they can have a low opinion of themselves because they are constantly expecting others to define them. High-functioning kids may be secretly afraid that if others knew the truth about them, they would see past their performances and realize that there is nothing much there.

Child or adult, it doesn't matter: in order to grow, we need to like ourselves. We must like ourselves separate from others' opinions. An accurate definition of self-esteem is: *self-esteem is what you think of yourself in spite of your performance and other people's opinions.*

There are no shortcuts here. Many people have tried to get around this journey by being nice, generous, successful, well liked, or by reading books about how much God loves them, in hopes something will build their self-esteem. This just doesn't work long term. These people usually just become more impressed that God could love someone as unlikable as they are, but they usually don't start liking themselves. It just doesn't translate into self-esteem. Remember the iconic old hymn?

> *"Amazing grace, how sweet the sound*
> *that saved a wretch like me ..."*

If wretch in this context is a synonym for *broke*n or *humbled*, it can be an important factor to the beginning of recovery. It is important to replace arrogance with humility in the recovery process. However, those in recovery must eventually find something to like about themselves. It might mean that they need to hit bottom and be torn down first, but then they need to be built up again with a new identity. "A wretch like me," has a theological foundation, but in the field of mental health, people who were once humbled need to see themselves as valuable and precious in order to grow or heal.

Ironically, seeing ourselves as exceptional does not seem to help self-esteem. It's more helpful to consider ourselves as not extraordinary, but just wonderful. The terms *normal* and *wonderful* show the paradox needed for self-esteem to exist. A good way to think about it is: *I love who I am but I know I'm no better than anyone else.*

THE FOUNDATIONS OF SELF-ESTEEM

Here is what is needed for self-love: love from someone else, accurate self-assessment, resilience, achievement, and the belief that we are not exceptional. A healthy self-love leads to self-esteem. Let's look at these important foundations.

1. Love

The first requirement for self-esteem is for a child to know someone loves him. It's hard for kids who have never known love to make it out of childhood grounded. This is immensely important. The only reason we are not devoting more pages to this is most parents do a good job of loving their kids. Probably even a higher percentage of those reading a book about parenting love their kids.

We've heard a lot of various complaints from kids, but we have never heard a kid complain that his/her parent says, "I love you," too much. The body language of kids may show indifference, but if they hear this frequently it still penetrates inside of them and fills their souls.

Loving your child immensely is definitely part of the self-esteem foundation.

Love must be present,
but it also must be convincing.

Love for a child happens in your heart. You know it's there but others may not be as sure. Kids can easily play the "no one loves me" tapes in their heads. This happens all the time. Just know it can take some artistry to convey the love you carry for your child. Love must be present, but it also must be convincing.

The most important factor in showing love is demonstrating utter joy that your child exists. This is also the most efficient way to show love and efficiency is an important part of good parenting.

When your daughter comes down in the morning or your son comes home after school, do your face and eyes show joy and gratitude that this child is in your life? You will have a tough time convincing a child you love him if your face reflects a dislike or disdain for him. In fact, it likely won't happen. You might know you still love him but your child is not going to believe it. It is nearly impossible for a child to believe he is loved if he also believes a parent regrets he exists.

Start with the look in your eyes when you are conveying love. Then move on to other ways to show love for your kids:

- Spend time with them

- Prove that you know who they are and what they are like

- Give evidence that they are nearly always on your mind

- Be firm and adult in your decisions

- Look out for their best interests, not for their requests or demands

- Value their opinions and privileges, but you don't need to agree

- Find different ways to refer to them as one of the blessings of your life

It is important that you decide how you are going to show love. Take into consideration who your child is and decide on your approach. As time goes on, it is OK for you to change your approach, but it won't work if you let your child change your approach. That will become a powerful and manipulative tool for your child's arsenal.

We want to say this as emphatically as we can. *Do not listen to what your child tells you he or she needs to feel loved.* This is a trap. You will be far better off following the list above, or any list you would like to make on your own.

THE LOVE TRAP

The simple love trap may sound like this, "If you loved me, you would let me sleep over at Donny's tomorrow night." A more complicated version would be, "If you loved me, you would get me back on Adderall so I can study." Or, the most confusing comes from a divorce situation: "If you loved me you wouldn't make me go to Mom's for the weekend" (You may not want your son to go to his mom's for various reasons, but that wouldn't be an "if you love me" issue).

Somewhere inside your child, she wants you to be in charge. Your daughter knows she needs help growing up. Your son knows that left on his own, he would ruin his life or at least his high school experience. As much as it may appear to the contrary, they want you to be an adult.

It is sad to hear a twenty-year-old say in counseling, "Looking back on it, I don't believe my parents loved me enough to stop me from smoking pot and sleeping around in high school." This is sad because this same young woman has probably forgotten that when she was sixteen, she screamed at her parents saying, "If you loved me you would get off my back." She probably said it with such power and conviction that her mom and dad might have partially believed she was right and gave her more space.

One of the most frequent themes in the love trap might sound similar to this: "If you loved me, you would respect me and my privacy and stay out of my room." This is one of the most familiar cries of today's adolescents. We don't recommend checking your child's room if you have no reason to suspect them of anything. Don't just go in and read your daughter's journal. But, definitely check her room if you have a reason to suspect something. Every day your child is living with a secret is another day she or he is not growing. Those days add up.

It is unwise to buy into your child's thinking on this issue. The "respect my privacy" argument, despite all the conviction and indignation it is expressed with, is mostly nonsense. Thousands of occupations require that an employee get tested, searched, watched, or recorded. Landlords in apartment buildings can go in and check a building they suspect to be in violation any time they have cause. If an apartment manager hears a bark coming from a building where dogs aren't allowed, the manager may go in and check for a dog when the tenant is not home. Dishonest, disrespectful, and suspicious behavior erodes your child's right to privacy.

The "respect my privacy" argument is mostly nonsense.

The problem here has nothing to do with love. It has to do with kids who want their rights respected when they don't want to respect the rights of others. If your son is worthy of respect, by all means respect every aspect of his life that you can. Checking a room has to do with respect, not love.

How are you going to express your love for your child? Take into account your child's interests and passions. If your son is on a diet, don't bake cookies to show your love for him. If your daughter is not athletic, don't take her on a strenuous hike. These expressions should be efficient and simple. You don't have to build a two-story tree house to express your love. The time increment that love comes in is moments. Commit to practicing these expressions. This is a commitment you make to yourself, not one you make to your child. Love your child in a way that is consistent with the commitment you have made to yourself.

As we have said before, love is expressed best one-on-one. As parents, we probably overvalue family time as it pertains to expressing love. For thirty years we have asked people about their best family memories and usually their best memory has nothing to do with the entire family. Most often it was time they spent alone with someone in the family. A son may say, "I remember the time my dad took me camping, just him and me." A daughter might say, "My mom and I went to a spa together and had the best time ever." Love penetrates a child best when his or her siblings are not around.

Focus more on your love for your child and less on your relationship with your child. Love is far more stable and predictable than relationships. Your child has the power to ruin her relationship with you, but she cannot ruin your love for her.

Over focusing on your relationship will hand your child too much power over you since you are valuing a dynamic she can choose to destroy. In desperate times she will use this power to pillage your relationship because she knows how tightly you are clutching it.

**Focus more on your love for your child
and less on your relationship.**

You will make far better decisions as a parent if you focus on love instead of relationship. It might surprise all of us to examine how many times the loving thing to do in a situation is the very thing that could cost us closeness. Love your child enough to be willing to risk your relationship. You will be stronger and make better decisions, and the leverage your child could potentially have over you will be neutralized.

2. Self-Assessment

A second essential for building self-esteem is accurate self-assessment. Self-assessment is the skill of being able to accurately see yourself as you are apart from the input or opinions of others. Because of its importance to self-esteem, we devoted the previous chapter to discussion about accurate truth telling. It's extremely important that parents teach their children how to accurately assess themselves. This is not a topic parents think much about or usually teach their children. Many adults have no experience in using this skill in their own lives.

This takes practice but it is a job perfectly suited for parents. Parents are there day and night and can ask, "How did you see yourself in this situation?" Or, "How do you think you did?"

When you look at your child's report card you can say, "This is what your teacher says about how you are doing. However, I am more interested in how *you* think you're doing. Do you agree with your teacher's assessment?"

Or, "Do you see yourself as quiet in class?"

Or, you might ask, "How do you think you played today?"

Or, "How did your recital go? Would you say it was better or worse than your last performance?"

A child may say about a D on his report card, "I think I did fine." If that happens, the parent should just say, "I don't believe you are happy with this grade. I think you are just saying that to get out of work. But even if you are happy with a D, I am not. That isn't going to be acceptable to me."

Kids should be able to roughly assess how well they did on a school presentation, or how well they mowed the lawn, or even how in-shape they are physically.

We are finding that kids are not adequately developing this skill. It is amazing how much of a child's life can go by without him having many chances to accurately self-appraise. As a parent, celebrate any time your child assesses anything accurately. Developing this trait is crucial to self-esteem. We believe that it is far more important that your son can assess accurately how well he did on an English paper or shoveling the driveway than the actual proficiency in doing either of these tasks.

As parents, we inherently assess our own children in ways that are inaccurate as we see them through biased eyes and rose-colored glasses. The ability and willingness to honestly give our children accurate feedback is the exception to the rule in most households. After all, we want desperately for our children to succeed, excel, and be the best. We will stretch the truth and even lie about their abilities, performance, and character in ways that attempt to self-fulfill some prophecy. Yet, for our children to truly know how they did, *we* must know how they really did and then teach them the skill of seeing themselves accurately.

The exaggerated way parents see their kids may result in affirmations. Just as often, it results in parents being hypercritical because they see a higher potential in their children than is actually there.

A child with an accurate view of himself can go through rough waters.

People struggle with accepting the truth about themselves. It takes practice and grace to be willing to learn this skill. What deceives many parents is the myth of a self-fulfilling prophecy. Parents sometimes believe that if they pump up their child's self-esteem by telling him he is great and talented and able to do anything he wants to do in his life, then this child will miraculously become great and talented. This simply is not the case. In fact, it can backfire. Overshooting your assessment of your child has a better chance of stifling his growth than it has of accelerating growth. An increasing number of kids do not have a clue about their true abilities because they are confused by what they have heard from their parents for years.

The truth is the majority of children do not grow up to become professional athletes, virtuoso musicians, brain surgeons, or CEOs of large corporations. That is OK.

Self-esteem suffers when a child's view of himself is different from what is true. It is easier for a kid to be frightened and turn against an unknown self than one that is known, liked, and accurate. A child with an accurate view of himself can go through rough waters.

3. Resilience

If a child has healthy self-esteem he can say after moments of failure, "I'll just try it again," or "I'll start over," or "I'll be more prepared next fall." When kids don't have resilience, they become scared and tentative about life. Resilience is needed to be able to effectively do life, with or without self-esteem. Although previously mentioned, resilience is necessary for self-esteem so we are briefly including it here.

It can be said that self-esteem is best measured when accolades have ceased, achievement has failed, friends are gone, and the path is unclear. It is unlikely any of us would get through these times without resilience. Resilience teaches us that failure does not mean defeat.

Practice allows your child to develop resilience. This happens naturally in normal family life. A different mindset is needed to parent this way. Remember to be grateful when difficulties surround your child. Instead of showing discomfort as kids face setbacks, we can appreciate how needed these difficulties are for them to believe in themselves.

Self-esteem is best measured when accolades have ceased, achievement has failed, friends are gone, and the path is unclear.

Resilience is one of the hardest lessons to learn because it so often involves covering the same ground twice. We try and fail, and then need to try the same thing again to succeed. Having to rewrite an essay after your computer loses what you've written is a good example of this. These situations in life involve achievement with disappointment—tough lessons for all of us.

All you need to do to develop this trait is to celebrate resilience whenever it appears in your family. In homes where getting up is applauded more than being comforted after falling down, resilience will find its own life and energy.

4. Achievement

Achievement is also an essential part of self-esteem. We wish this were not true as it would really be a good progression if some kids could repair and raise their self-esteem first and then go out and tackle some achievement. However, achievement of some type must be part of self-esteem building. The most effective adolescent treatment programs we know of are programs that incorporate achievement into their treatment plan. The least effective are those that try to build self-esteem before achievement is established.

The achievements need to be personal. The kind of authentic self-esteem that can be built upon happens when a band member writes a good song, or a student perfects a role in a theater production. Any achievement that kids do solely to gain the approval of others has a more negligible effect on building self-esteem. In other words, an achievement that originates with your son's passion is going to be a building block of self-esteem. But, an achievement that originates from his obedience, conforming, or submission will have a much smaller impact.

If you have a higher functioning child you may not relate to this because your child's life is full of achievements. For many others, there may not be a significant achievement to be noticed anywhere. If you are the parent of one of these kids, you will know exactly how difficult this hurdle can be to clear. Innumerable kids have functioned so poorly in life—hanging out, using drugs, or skipping school—for so long they literally have not had an achievement in months.

Anyone attempting to help a child with low self-esteem needs to keep in mind that without an accomplishment of some type this is an uphill struggle at best. These kids do not need to bring food to Haiti after an earthquake, or spend two nights alone in the wilderness, even though these are noble ideas. But, fixing the family's computer, adding two new apps to Mom's smartphone, driving a little sister to swimming, or getting caught up on missing math assignments will all qualify as small starting points.

If a child you love is stuck, make sure he has achieved something in the recent past. If he has not, success in gaining self-esteem will be nominal.

5. The Myth of Specialness

There is an epidemic of *gifted* children in developed countries. The topic of gifted children shows up in hockey rinks, in math class, at Starbuck's, in parent-teacher conferences, and other places parents congregate. A growing percentage of kids today are thought to be gifted; however, that cannot be true.

Let's look at the discipline of probability theory. This theory again says there are a known number of gifted children out of every hundred children. What is known and true is that about 68.27 percent of those measured on any trait lie within one standard deviation of the mean. Similarly, about 95.45 percent of the values lie within two standard deviations of the mean. That means, by definition, 4.55 percent of kids lie outside two standard deviations to the high and to the low end. Take out the half on the low end, and this leaves about 2.27 percent of the population to be above average in any measurable trait. Think of it as 97.73 percent fall below the gifted line. Bottom line: most kids are not gifted.

Something has shifted in our culture. It has now become unacceptable in some vague way *not* to be gifted. To be normal is to be below. We can deny it or argue about it, but anyone who works with kids can feel the undertow around them. Parents are baffled and angry that their child didn't make an elite traveling basketball team. Kids may feel disappointed because they only got a ninety-two percent on an English paper. Increasingly, parents see normal or average as an unacceptable reality for their children. There is no doubt the kids are feeling it. As a result, more kids than ever express the desire to give up if they don't excel at something.

> **When kids feel average is an insult,**
> **they will aspire to being gifted,**
> **instead of working to be effective.**

Kids who are not exceptional in math feel they are less than those who are gifted. Girls without an exceptional figure hate the way they look. When kids today say, "I'm not good at anything," what they mean is that they are not exceptional at anything. These kids are finding it increasingly difficult to take comfort in being just like most of the rest of us.

This should be a wonderful reality. If I am ordinary, I fit in. I am no better or worse than anyone else. Most of the greatest people in history were not gifted people in any innate way; they were normal. From their normality they were able to achieve important and exceptional things. Normal kids need to embrace their normality, not fight it. If kids continue to feel defective because they are not exceptional, healthy self-esteem is going to be elusive and fleeting.

In our culture, when gifted becomes expected, normal becomes defective. It is an important aspect of growth, peace, and self-esteem that the core of who we are is good enough. Inside, people need to believe that their core self is something they can be happy with. It is actually all they have to be happy with. When kids feel that average is an insult they will aspire to being gifted instead of working to be effective. Self-esteem takes an unnecessary hit when this pointless weight is placed upon our kids.

What if your child is truly in the upper two percent of kids in a certain skill or trait? We still recommend you be careful about pushing this perception on your child. It is fine to mention this so your child understands your expectations that she work at a level commensurate with her ability. Any more than this will not be helpful. Here's why. If your child ends up going to MIT, most likely she will be quite average in that setting. What if your MIT candidate tries waterskiing? She might be quite average in that setting also. Being able to feel comfortable with being average is a great trait for us all to learn. Fortunately most of us *are* average, so it is just a matter of accepting the truth.

WONDERFUL IS FULFILLING; EXCEPTIONAL IS DRAINING.

It is an excellent idea to ask someone with average skills to do a credible and admirable job on something. Just do not expect them to be gifted if they are not. There is so much unrest and tendencies to quit in kids. A part of this is because they feel their family and culture only value the exceptional. Remember, only about 2.27 percent of the population is exceptional on any given identifiable trait. We, as a culture, need to start celebrating the wonderful achievements of normal kids.

The Story of Peter

Peter was a *boy* who was about to turn twenty. During most of the previous five years of his life he just existed and used—pot, Adderall improperly, alcohol, video games. He slept in, skipped school, and hung out. To understand how Peter got to this condition would take about eighty pages of this book. Surprisingly to some, Peter got this way with two loving parents and a good home.

Peter could argue with the masters. He had a fierce temper. He had a much stronger persona than either parent. His parents primarily just wanted everyone to get along. "Why can't we get along?" they'd ask and "Why can't Peter just do what he's supposed to do?" There were no answers on the horizon.

When he was fifteen, he realized his athletic skills, which had served him well until this age, were no better than average. Kids with average athleticism have no place to go in organized sports after fifteen. He started vigorously pursuing video games. *World of Warcraft* became an obsession in tenth and eleventh grades. This contributed to his grades dropping. He began to lose friends in the real world, friends he replaced in cyberspace.

Early in the eleventh grade, Peter hit a plateau in his gaming. Though he was good at it he realized that he wasn't exceptional in the video gaming world either. He had easily climbed levels in several games, but then found it harder and harder to achieve *legend* status amongst his cyber friends. In sports and in gaming, Peter wanted to be exceptional. When he realized he was just average, that would not do.

Peter got bored with the video experience and started watching movies incessantly. The few people he associated with were beginning to drink and smoke pot. Peer pressure got to him. In addition, the best stories going around school all involved someone being plastered or wasted. If you wanted to be in the best stories, you knew what you had to do.

Peter had distanced himself from his parents since his video game season. He had to. Initially, to keep playing four hours a day, he had to lie about his grades and his homework. Then he had to lie about the lies. Before long he was vague about life in general, stayed secluded in his room, was angry with his parents, and was generally uncooperative.

His parents saw their son slipping away. When either parent tried to reach out to him, Peter would pull further away. When his dad asked Peter to help a little around the house, Peter would see it as an injustice and shut down even more. If his parents left him alone and asked nothing from him, he would hang out in the kitchen and make a snack, carry in some groceries, or watch an old "House" rerun with his mom and dad. This was all they had left of their relationship with Peter. They didn't want to do anything to jeopardize what little was left.

By then, Peter hated himself. He had alienated his parents, so he was unable to benefit from their love. He did not respect his loser friends. He often needed to medicate himself to face the day. He had not achieved anything of value for many months and he had totally lost track of who he was. Peter's self-esteem was in a free fall, but it had never been high in the first place. He had created his own prison. While serving time in that prison, he had fallen far behind his well-functioning peers and had not learned the skills needed to embark on a different path.

Peter's story is common. He knew his parents loved him, but, other than that, he had none of the building blocks needed for self-esteem. He had poor self-assessment, no resilience, and no achievements derived from his own passions. He didn't believe he was valued.

He quit sports and video games when he realized that he was average. His parents were average and they were fine with Peter being average, but in Peter's culture average was not OK. In the upper-middle class suburb where he grew up there were subtle and implied messages everywhere that normal would not be good enough. Signs about excellence hung over the entry of the school and were printed in size forty-eight font on the title page of his school's yearbook. With over 600 students in his graduating class, Peter felt if he were not exceptional at something he would just be part of the masses walking the halls and that made him feel desolate.

Fortunately, Peter was able to grow. In time, he learned to like himself. This was achieved by slowly chipping away at his low self-esteem by actively listening to him and repairing his misperceptions about his world.

"How Do You Think You Did?"

Some parents don't believe their child could give an accurate critique of himself, and they are probably right. We encourage parents to ask their child, "How do you think you did?" on a regular basis whether it's regarding a report card, basketball game, crayon drawing, or mowing the lawn. A child with good self-esteem will gradually answer more honestly and accurately. The job of the parent is to either confirm the child's assessment or guide him to reassess if he's off-track. If your son ever said, "I did an average job on the lawn," you as the parent should pay more attention to the accuracy of his self-assessment than the quality of his mowing.

Ultimately, we do not create self-esteem in our children by affirming them to death. We only perpetuate their false sense of self and we may even fuel their dependency on the esteem of others.

In America, it is hard to imagine young ladies having any self-esteem at all around an issue like body image. Hollywood, TV shows, and clothing models give girls the message they will only be accepted if they look like *that*. This impacts the self-esteem of most American young women.

If we are to teach our children self-assessment and how to look at themselves as they are, truthfully and realistically, it must begin with us. We must tell our kids the realities of their lives: their talents, their intelligence, their true abilities, and their weaknesses. Yes, even their weaknesses. This does not mean we should focus on what they cannot do, but instead guide them on a path that fits who they are.

The GIST of It

- The addictive nature of needing the esteem of others is at the core of our children's low self-esteem.

- The esteem of others feels like self-esteem, but it is significantly different.

- Love, accurate self-assessment, resilience, and achievement will instill self-esteem in your child.

- Don't buy into our culture's message that your children need to be exceptional and gifted. It simply is not true. Normal kids are unique and wonderfully made.

CHAPTER SIXTEEN:

SHAME

Shame is one of the silent destroyers of families in our country and around the world. We define it as the painful sense that we have lost value as a person because of poor performance, bad behavior, or a mistake. Shame is the primary reason that so few kids live a balanced life. Everyone, to some degree, will battle shame in their lives.

The spectrum of shame goes from mild to severe and can vary in its effect. Mild shame causes tears and anger. It makes apologizing difficult and defensiveness a certainty. In younger kids it is at the core of bullying and teasing. It is at the heart of what drives a class clown. Shame is why a teen might squeal his tires or fail a test.

More significant shame is behind anorexia nervosa, much drug use, sexual misconduct, and is a significant contributor to obesity. It can be the reason someone joins a gang, drops out of school, stays in an abusive relationship, or becomes the abuser in a relationship. Shame is at the center of chemical and alcohol addiction, and it is a primary reason for experimenting with and using drugs.

Understanding the origins of shame is critical to effective and healthy parenting. From our perspective, a major goal of parenting is to raise what we call shame-reduced kids. We say shame-reduced because it is doubtful that a child can grow up "shame free" in our culture. The goal is to parent without adding to cultural shame, and ideally, to even neutralize some of it.

THE GOOD OLD DAYS

Shame has been around for a long time. To understand the role that shame plays in our history, let's look at parenting back in what some call the "good old days." Those good old days—back two, three and four generations—were good for some reasons. In a more rural and agrarian society, kids felt needed. Not necessarily special, just needed. They were essential to the care of the farm. In urban society, teens would work long hours and turn their paychecks in to the family to help pay bills and buy food, maybe keeping for themselves five percent. Kids grew up respecting their elders and knew what a hard day of work felt like. Years ago, kids saw higher levels of school as a privilege, instead of a requirement or an entitlement. They knew it was a blessing to be able to go to school past the eighth grade. Generations ago a variety of body types were seen as beautiful or acceptable.

That said, the good old days were rife with shame. Kids were hit and belittled. Teasing was as bad as it is today; it just took a different form. Kids spoke respectfully to their elders, but they often didn't respect those elders. They just spoke respectfully out of fear of getting slapped if they didn't. Kids of previous generations did much of what they did because they didn't think they deserved any better. It was not uncommon for adults to work their whole lives in a coal mine, farm a hopeless piece of clay soil, or stay in a marriage that was painful and doomed from the beginning.

There have been extensive and far-reaching changes to life in the past thirty years as there have been far reaching changes to childhood. One thing that hasn't changed is shame. Shame looked different in our grandparent's era, but in studying history we see that deep shame has been around forever. This is not a new battle. It has just taken on a new face with the passing of time and new technology.

It may be more appropriate to define the good old days as just *different* days. Glamorizing the past serves no purpose and is just rewriting history.

THE IMPACT OF SHAME

An understanding of shame is critically important to good parenting. Shame often controls what we do and how we see ourselves. Shame is often behind the following traits:

- Low self-esteem and low self-worth. When you believe you are bad at your core, it's hard to feel good about yourself.

- Feeling like you're not good enough. When you live in shame, you do not feel you deserve success, caring friends, or other good things.

- Low self-confidence. When you believe that you are not capable, you will hold back, not believing you can achieve your dreams.

- Believing you are bad. When you have identified punishment with being bad at your core, you believe you are no good.

We live in a shame-based culture, with significant amounts

of overt and covert shaming going on. This makes it a challenge to have a shame-free childhood or be shame-free as an adult. Commercials tell us we deserve the best. This shames those who can't get the best or don't have the best. The media endlessly project thin and beautiful women with perfect complexions, shaming young women for their variety of shapes and looks. Mutual fund commercials show a sixty-year-old man who has just retired pulling up in front of his multi-million dollar home or sailing a $400,000 sailboat. These media messages all contain shaming messages, but it's a passive sort of shame.

A shaming message makes someone feel defective when that person is just fine the way he or she is. Passive shame is sneaky. Everyone who doesn't have what everyone else has or look how they're "supposed" to look or act like they're "supposed" to act or dress like they're "supposed" to dress is covertly shamed. Of course, it is up to the individual to fend off that message, but it isn't always easy unless they understand what is happening.

Our culture clearly defines the *haves* and the *have-nots*. We have private schools for those affluent enough for that option. Even in public schools, the differences are obvious. Some kids get $7,000 four-wheelers for their birthdays or new cars when they turn sixteen, not to mention an iPad or trips to Mexico and Europe during high school. These kids may sit next to a kid in math class who still watches a tube TV at home and gets some of their clothes from a consignment shop. There is nothing wrong with any of these life situations. But, teens who "don't have" can feel perpetually faulty and deficient.

We see kids in our professional practices who feel they need certain possessions in order not to be humiliated at school for falling too far behind the baseline when it comes to accumulating stuff. All parents and educators can do is to play a role in minimizing shame.

Shame is different from remorse in the way it is being used here. Remorse, or healthy guilt, is an appropriate sense that I have done something wrong. It would be great if a student who cheated on a science test felt guilty about what he or she did. In fact, it is a great concern if the student doesn't feel remorse or have a bad conscience about it.

It's healthy to:

- Feel remorse that I made the family late,
- Feel regret that I didn't keep a promise, or
- Feel contrite that I lied about turning in an assignment.

How Shame Works in the Mind

Everyone is a partly good and partly bad person (with very few exceptions). All people can be giving at times and remarkably selfish at other times. We all have some attractive features, but we all know somebody better looking than we are. Everyone has let a friend down and, at some other point, come through big time for a friend. Everyone has lost his temper and also exhibited incredible grace and forgiveness during the course of his lifetime.

Those who work with inmates in prison may be amazed by the kindness and intelligence of some of those men and women. Contrast that with the ignorance and control that can be exhibited by CEOs or religious leaders. We all live somewhere in the middle. The bottom line is: You're not as good as you think you are on your best days and you're not as bad as you think you are on your worst days. We need to recognize that reality and admit it.

An interviewer once asked Mother Theresa: "What would be most surprising to an outsider if he watched you every day and got to know you?" Mother Theresa replied that an outsider would be surprised at how normal and unremarkable she was.

Yes, we all live in the middle. Sometimes we fall on our faces and sometimes we bring a much-needed ray of light to a situation. That is the nature of life and the nature of self-honesty. But, knowing and accepting this is difficult when someone is haunted by shame.

Shame: Living in the Extremes

At the core of most people's shame is a sense of feeling somewhat defective. When children mix up what they have done with who they are, they come away feeling either arrogant or defective. They may feel as if they have passed the test, beat the odds, and become a model for what life should look like. Or, they feel they have fallen short, are inadequate, and less than they need to be to have standing with others in their peer group.

By its nature shame is extreme. Shame will not let us live in the middle as a partly good and partly bad person. It tells us that falling short or making a mistake or having a bad trait is evidence we are not good enough. This sense of feeling defective causes us to hide and defend our mistakes.

Shame can look either positive or negative in different people. Those who live in a *positive shame cycle* endlessly try to live better, perform better, and not let others down. They frequently become perfectionists in order to hide how they really feel about themselves.

When someone is in a positive shame cycle she aspires to be kind, smart, attractive, responsible, giving, brave, competent, or whatever qualities she happens to value. This is always at the price of self-honesty. On these occasions she actually believes this is what accurately describes her. In this state, she ignores how controlling, angry, self-centered, unforgiving, and judgmental she is. Convinced that she has made the grade, she believes the world would be a better place with more people like her.

Conversely, a shamed-based person in a *negative shame cycle* believes or feels she is unattractive, stupid, disliked, afraid, lazy, or incompetent. In this state the person ignores her generosity, accomplishments, kindness, popularity, and any other aspect of "goodness." She deflects compliments and does not see any achievement as *good enough*. Those who live in a negative shame cycle try to hide, defend, and blame away their mistakes as a maladaptive way to fend off feeling defective.

> **The person in a positive shame cycle
> consistently denies her *badness*.
> The person in a negative shame cycle denies
> her *goodness*.**

Both the person in a positive shame cycle and the one in the negative shame cycle are driven by shame. The starting quarterback and the valedictorian can be equally as shame-driven as a drop-out or gang member. In this environment there is no rest and no peace. Why? Because, the truth is, we all live in the middle. In shame cycles, shame has in effect taken away the middle, so life never feels quite right.

In a sense, shame whispers in our ear that we are either wonderful or awful, and we must decide each moment. This is why shame-based people can shift from feeling superior to feeling defective as fast as it takes to utter a foolish comment or slip on the ice.

The techniques and parenting approaches shared in this book are designed to minimize shame while still holding our kids to high standards and discipline. In life, shame usually comes from words, either self-talk or words from another source or person. Normally, change comes from our experiences, not from talking. This is why we cannot emphasize enough the importance of a parenting approach that includes as little discussion about mistakes as possible.

Consequences change behavior and talking fosters shame.

Many parents think it is profitable to have a "nice long talk" about what went wrong Friday night or why homework wasn't turned in. We believe these talks should be as short as possible, perhaps thirty seconds or less. Perhaps there should be no discussion at all. Here is an important point in good parenting: For the most part, consequences change behavior and talking fosters shame.

Molly's Story

Molly is a fourteen-year-old partly good and partly bad kid who is living life in the middle. She asked her mom if she could go to the mall with Lindsey and Steph. Her mother agreed and Molly and her friends were off for the day. Molly promised her mom that she would not go anywhere else.

At the mall, Molly, Lindsey, and Steph met up with some boys and the five of them decided to go across the parking lot to a pizza place to connect with another group of friends they heard might be in the area. It might not sound like a big deal, but Molly had specifically guaranteed her mother she would only be at the mall and only with her two friends. She was to call home if there was any change in the plan; but she didn't call.

Her mom found out, of course. One of mom's friends called her up to chat a little and mentioned in passing, and with no malicious intent, that she had seen Molly with a group of friends at the pizza place. When Molly returned home, her mom confronted her. Caught off guard and not knowing of the call from her mother's friend, Molly lied about what happened. Her mom understandably felt disrespected by Molly's dishonesty and believed her deception merited a consequence. Molly's mom took her cell phone away and grounded her for four days, and then instructed Molly to go to the family office for a talk.

Once in the office, her mom explained the whole story of how she found out about the "deception." Then she talked about how Molly had changed in the last six months. She said another mom had made comments about Molly's hair and makeup that weren't good. The friend also said, "Molly doesn't smile like she used to and she's choosing different clothes. What's going on?"

Molly's mom went on to tell her daughter, "You started changing a few months ago. Your grades started dropping, and you've been really mean to your little brother.

"I hoped you wouldn't lie to me when I asked you about the day," she said. "How could you sit there with a straight face and blatantly lie? How could you do that to me? I am so tired of all of this. I can't trust you anymore and I feel so bad."

Molly stormed out of the "talk" and said to her mother, "You are a freakin' ninja parent! I hate you and you are ruining my whole life! Thanks a lot!"

This true story is typical. Some parenting books recommend having these talks. We believe these talks are unproductive and a way that shame is added to Molly's life. Molly walked away from this thirty-minute talk feeling like a complete failure. Her grades were bad, her room was a mess, she was a liar, and her friend choices were poor. Heck, she wasn't even smiling the right way anymore.

To minimize shame for Molly, her mom could have handled this situation differently. It might have sounded something like this:

"Molly, my friend mentioned she saw you with a bunch of friends at the pizza shack yesterday. I don't know that you were or weren't doing anything wrong there. I just know that isn't what we agreed would happen yesterday. As I recall, we agreed that any change in the plan would need to include calling me. This isn't a big deal to me, but you are going to need to stay home this weekend. Then starting Monday morning we will be back to normal."

This message is saying: "I'm not commenting whether I do or don't trust you, I'm just saying you broke our agreement this afternoon."

This response simply addresses what Molly did to be grounded. There is no grouping of issues, no speculation about wrongdoing, and no discussion about Molly's whole life becoming a disaster. Besides minimizing shame, this is simply a more efficient and effective way to parent. This is the type of comment that will result in the greatest probability of Molly changing for the positive.

Molly's mom is a loving mother, but she was fooled into thinking that Molly would be more likely to change if she told her all the areas of failure in her life in the past couple of months. This is a common mistake. It happens when loving, conscientious, but misguided parents aren't sure what is happening before their very eyes. Second, it comes from the belief that Molly doesn't feel bad enough about who she has become for her to change.

It is understandable that Molly's mom would conclude this. Molly didn't look sorry—and indeed wasn't sorry—for anything she did that day. In triggering Molly's shame, Mom caused Molly to need to defend her soul and character. Molly's defensiveness reinforced her mother's belief that Molly didn't see what a different child she had become. So, Mom tried to bring in the unrelated issues about her grades, her room, her honesty, her kindness, and her smile, all of which had declined.

This approach will never convince Molly to see things she should be concerned about. That isn't what Molly needed. She needed to know that she broke the agreement and will be staying home for the weekend. That is all.

MINIMIZING SHAME

Always remember that your kids live in a world that heaps shame on them from many directions. How you talk to them will either add to it or help reduce it. Honest, straightforward, simple, and brief communications regarding their mistakes is the best way to reduce shame in their lives. Keep it simple and to the point. Don't contaminate it with other issues that are unrelated. Stay with a reasonable consequence and follow through. Finally, be hopeful in what you say. Convey to them that what they did doesn't change your love for them. It is not the end of the world, and life will soon return to normal.

The GIST of It

- Shame is the painful feeling of having lost value as a person from a mistake, a comparison, a put down, or a limitation. We feel *diminished* when we are doing just fine or when we have made a normal human mistake.

- Guilt involves healthy remorse. It is the appropriate feeling after an error. Guilt does not threaten our value or our worth the way shame does. With shame we feel diminished or *less than*.

- Most shame comes from careless words that contribute to people feeling defective and deficient.

- Shame usually functions as either a positive shame cycle or a negative shame cycle. In a positive shame cycle, people look and perform very well as a means to fend off the defectiveness they feel. In a negative shame cycle, people give up or make poor choices as they surrender to their perceived defectiveness.

- We are all partly good and partly bad; we all need to learn to live in the middle of that reality. Shame will not allow us to live in the middle.

- The only way to heal from shame is to simultaneously embrace our flaws and our wonder. We are never totally good or totally bad. We are never a total mess or totally together. When we learn to accept this we have a chance of healing from shame and living with the peace that the middle brings.

Chapter Seventeen:

Over-Parenting

The child characters in the movie *Charlie and the Chocolate Factory* show us some interesting things about parenting. Augustus is an obese candy addict who never stops obsessing about food. His plump mother is his source and supplies him on demand. His eating has become his identity, the way for his mom to keep him happy, and the only connection he has with her.

Violet is very cocky and a proud world-champion gum chewer. Her trophy cases are filled with dozens of medals and trophies. Her mother has spent much time affirming her and has ingrained in Violet the thought that she "is the best."

Next is Verruca (which means wart) who is a very wealthy spoiled girl whose father has never said the word "No" to her. She successfully demands anything and everything from her father. We quickly learn to dislike this entitled child for having no sense of delayed gratification.

And then there's Mike. He is addicted to media, especially video games. For him, stimulation is everything and violence is the outcome. While inside the factory Mike destroys a pumpkin-shaped candy creation, taking great pleasure in the process. His father stands by watching, incapable of dealing with his son's show of unprovoked violence.

The last kid, and main character, is Charlie, a sweet young boy from a very poor and destitute family. His father works hard and makes little. He lives in a dilapidated house with his parents and four elderly grandparents. He shares a special relationship with all of them, especially one grandfather who used to work at the chocolate factory. His family is the most important thing he has. He has a gift of wisdom far beyond his years and shares all that he has with those he loves. He ties no conditions to these relationships and is grateful for what little he has, even cabbage soup.

Of course, the characters in the movie are all exaggerations. Charlie knows who he is and where he and his family fit into the world around him. All of the "things" the other children have or are given by their parents pale in comparison to what Charlie knows he has: a family that loves him, a heart for people, and a peace about his life's condition. He simply is himself, not trying to perform or impress, not trying to get more for himself. He needs no praise for his behavior.

The other children are examples of over-parenting—one of the most common mistakes parents make. Just like when we over-do anything else, over-parenting takes over our lives and results in an unhealthy family system. Too often our instinct to become involved, affirm, indulge, and protect becomes a mission to keep our children far away from the truth about themselves and the reality of their life and world.

1. The Mistake of Over-Involvement

We believe in parenting as little as possible. By this we mean to wear your parenting hat as little as possible. We all do things around the house, run errands, and engage in activities where we are not functioning as parents. Most of us want to be involved and engaged parents, but there are times when our children are doing just fine. You may have a child who is polite enough, eats well enough, studies just enough, helps out around the house just barely enough, has pretty good friends, and goes to bed without a scene. This is the type of kid who just needs you to sit back and enjoy his growth. Many parents keep parenting this kind of child when things are going along quite nicely without any needed intervention.

The first time your child won't come in when you call him for supper, just go ahead and eat without him. Until this pattern repeats itself and becomes a problem, there is no need to do anything.

We know numerous parents who have pretty good kids and would only need to parent a few hours a month, and yet they are parenting eight to ten hours a day. This is over-parenting.

It usually starts with a parent being overly critical for no apparent reason. When the parent senses intuitively that she has been picking on a relatively good kid, she may try to offset the critical comments with praise and affirmations. Praise will never offset our being critical. We need to stop pretending that it will.

Kids need to be left alone when they are functioning well. In our offices we have asked many parents these simple questions: "What grade point average would your child need to maintain in school for you to sign a contract saying you agree never to mention homework, studying, or school again?" Or "Would you agree to never mention homework if your daughter or son maintained a 3.7 grade point average?" The answer, nearly every time, is, "I would never agree to that. I don't care how well my child is doing; I want the right to talk to him about school."

Praise will never offset our being critical.

This same pattern carries over to a dozen other areas, including discussions about food choices, how clean a bedroom is, how the dishwasher is loaded, a situation on the school bus, a baseball breaking a neighbor's window, or who is to blame in a sibling squabble. Needlessly parenting when nothing needs to be done is over-parenting and sometimes borders on harassment. It is parenting when nothing is wrong or parenting when the child has the situation well under control.

If the child needs your help, fine, but if he is handling the broken window on his own, why get involved? That would be over-parenting.

Let kids have their lives, their school, their friends, their dilemmas, and their solutions. If it isn't working, step in. A great question to ask would be, "About that window you broke next door, take it as far as you can with Mr. Johnson, and then if you need any help, you can ask me." If the child is managing the situation, back away and see what happens. To do anything else is to over-parent.

A great question to ask your kid is, "What do you think you should do?" You'll never know how good an answer you might get if you don't ask.

2. The Mistake of Over-Affirmation

One over-parenting mistake we see many parents make is over-affirmation. This is rooted in our need to nurture. It can also be connected, subconsciously, to trying to offset being overly critical. Nurturing and affirming our children is fine, but too much of a good thing creates problems. Too much of a bad thing creates problems, too.

In the "Tell the Truth" chapter, we wrote about the risk of affirmations that are inaccurate. The caution about affirmations here focuses on simply over-using them. This can happen at the same time: too frequent and inaccurate affirmations.

Inaccurate over-affirmation tells Mary that she is the best gymnast in the competition even though she came in third. It tells Ryan he played better than everybody else at the piano recital even though he lost his place twice and botched the end of the piece.

Even accurate affirmations can become too repetitive. Early over-affirmations are found in and outside the home. Observe the posters often displayed in our elementary schools with their positive messages about how great every student is. When part of a child's world is saturated with affirmation, most of those affirmations become mute white noise to the kid and self-esteem is not built in the child. It becomes an expected and repetitive part of each day.

Children track how many compliments and accolades they receive compared to the other kids in the class and compare them to what they have received before. When they hear a constant flow of accolades and admiration, particularly when they have achieved nothing out of the ordinary, most of these comments are dismissed and the child does not internalize anything beneficial. This can become a silent or invisible quota for the child that needs to be met to get his attention. If a child is told he did well at something he puts it into a context of how many times he was told yesterday that he did well. He also weighs it against the number of compliments the other children his age received at school or in social settings at that particular time. Then the child evaluates it all to see if anything is worth letting into his spirit.

Parents reduce the chances of their hoped-for outcome by inundating a child with too frequent encouragement. To improve the effect of an affirmation, briefly give praise when it is merited and accurate.

Parents are hoping to nurture and develop their child's inner spirit when they overuse affirmation. The best way to accomplish this is to simply watch, and enjoy your child with your full attention. Saying, "I had so much fun watching you build that fort," is a far better way to nurture than saying, "That is the best fort ever!" This gives the child what he really wants: to know he is important to you and that he brings you joy. This can be accomplished with silence or minimal words. This is a message they can see in your eyes. Telling them that a mediocre fort is the "best fort ever" will not achieve this goal and will hurt a parent's credibility.

Comparative words are often used instinctively in accolades. These are words like, "best, more than, or better than." It is easy to use these words in a compliment. But over time these comments can become more destructive than helpful. Every person has the opportunity to learn, train, practice, strive, and work toward goals in life. When a child does anything worth noting, briefly mention that you noticed something admirable about what he did, without comparing it to other children or that child's past.

Parents give compliments to their kids hoping to offset too much recent criticism. The parent may have a brief awareness that he has been too critical or hard on his child one evening and tries to balance these harsh remarks with affirmations. This doesn't work and will only cause *feedback overload*. You can't balance too much criticism. It is better to own your mistake and admit it to your daughter or son. Then apologize without compromising your affirmations by trying to balance the scale.

Remember, a constant banter of affirmations and encouragement is not helpful and doesn't even mean that much to a child. Part of why precious metals are valuable is because they are rare. Flooding the market with a million tons of gold would depreciate its value. It is the same thing with constant, unfocused accolades that are said to kids on a normal day when they have done nothing out of the ordinary. This depreciates the affirming comments.

A significant consequence of over-affirmation for a child is the inability to honestly assess himself. When parents overuse accurate affirmations, kids will start to expect them. If the frequency of those true affirmations decreases, the child begins to wonder what's wrong with him. "Why isn't Mom telling me how well I'm doing at school?" It's not just false affirmations that are harmful. Over-saying "I'm proud of you," even if it's true, is not helpful and adds stress to a child's life.

3. The Dangers of Over-Indulgence

Over-indulgence is another form of over-parenting and is rooted in our culture's message that to be the best parents we need to give everything to our kids.

We live in an abundant society. We want many things yet need little. Some have more than others and some have less. That's OK. Our culture tells us that our children deserve it all and need it now. The list of indulgences is long enough to fill a book. A few of those things might be: $300 video game players, smartphones, American Girl dolls, iPods and iPads, motorized scooters, sports camps, dance lessons, $125 basketball shoes, Barbie cars, custom birthday parties, bedroom computers, limos to prom, and $90 jeans. The available choices today are staggering and have created an insatiable appetite for more in us and in our kids.

The consequence of over-indulgence is a child who feels entitled. This inability to delay gratification creates entitled young adults (and gets many of their parents into difficult financial situations). It's an ongoing battle not to buy for kids what everyone else already has. Jimmy just got a new X-Box in his bedroom. Kayla's mom bought her designer jeans. Corey's parents got him a car for his sixteenth birthday.

It's a counter-cultural message to teach our children that money doesn't grow on trees and that waiting is a good thing. Having it all now and at a young age hinders natural creativity in our children. They spend a lot of time looking and pining for the next new thing. They play less and lose their natural ability to be creative. Over-indulging our children steals the "child" out of childhood and creates the entitled generation we see today.

The Boredom Experiment

Imagine if parents actually allowed their children to get bored for five days over summer vacation. Let's say the parents decide to do the following experiment: no TV, no trips to the mall, no friends over, no technology, no swimming at the community center, and no video games for five days.

One family did this when their three kids were ages eleven, eight, and six. What happened was very interesting. For almost three days, the siblings complained and whined, but to no avail. On the third day, they decided to go outside and build a fort. And that's what they did. Together they searched for old two-by-fours and sheets of wood, tools, nails, screws, and glue. Then they found an acceptable tree in the woods across the street and started building. For two days they built. When they finished, it wasn't pretty, but it worked. It was sturdy and big enough. It was their creation and they were very proud of what they had accomplished. Most creations, like forts, start from boredom.

4. Over-Protection

Over-protection, the last piece of the over-parenting quartet, seems to be the most common. Parents who over-protect rarely let their kids fall down in life. In essence, they are the cushions always hovering beneath their child. The goal is to protect their child from experiencing the pain of life when he gets in trouble, doesn't make the team, or fails in some way.

These parents make excuses for their children when there's a potential for disappointment. Sometimes the excuses are directed at the child: "The coach has it in for you." Or, "Your team lost because the ref was terrible." Or, "You didn't get the lead in the musical because the director is good friends with Melanie's parents."

Sometimes the parent preemptively creates the outcome by chumming up to the coach during tryouts. This is a proactive form of over-protection. Then the child doesn't need to suffer the very normal and important part of life we call *disappointment*. Over-protection is rooted in a parent's need for his child to avoid pain, because when he hurts, the parent hurts.

The primary consequence of over-protection is dependency. These children are so conditioned to being bailed out that they are not able to cope with the adult world. Eventually their parents will not be there to protect them and they will crumble. Over-protecting a child may even cause some kids to grow up with a skewed and fearful view of the world.

Which one teaches us more about ourselves: success or failure? Is wisdom learned from everything going as we think it should or from our collisions with life? When children grow up over-protected, their emotional growth is hindered, and their ability to deal with adversity is greatly reduced. The resulting dependency on their parents when things get a little rough will prevent them from being self-sufficient adults. Letting our kids fall down and feel disappointment and pain in life is an essential part of good parenting. They need to learn how to deal with the things life deals them. The wonderful experiences of disappointment are invaluable opportunities for growth.

The GIST of It

- The over-parenting big four are: over-involvement, over-affirmation, over-indulgence, and over-protection.
- Kids with over-involved parents end up feeling controlled and resentful.
- Over-affirmed kids end up with an inaccurate picture of who they are.
- Over-indulged kids end up feeling entitled.
- Over-protected kids end up dependent.
- When your child is doing life well, just enjoy it. Compliments or criticism are simply not needed.

Part III

Unintended Parenting

CHAPTER EIGHTEEN:
BE CAREFUL WHAT YOU SAY

A t times we all speak in clichés. We mindlessly repeat unexamined platitudes or vent our frustrations without stopping to consider the effect of our words. As parents, we need to become more careful of our use of certain words and messages, particularly the messages we repeatedly convey to our kids or ourselves. Platitudes that have been passed down from previous generations may need to be reassessed. To make sure we understand what it is we are communicating, we need to re-think the messages we give our kids.

The first step in change is to be aware. First, we'll focus on two statements commonly used by parents that can have serious negative consequences. Because these statements are so pervasively used—although both are baseless—we'll address them specifically. Next we will look at the ineffective consequences of the use of threats, warnings, and reminders. Too many parents have an arsenal made up primarily of these parenting "tools." We recommend this arsenal of tools be eliminated from every parent's parenting toolbox, or at least minimized.

Finally, we will look at the dynamic of lashing out at our kids or unloading. We as parents need to be aware, prior to blow-ups or disappointments or moments of fear, of what messages we can't afford to say to our children. After we say them, we can't take them back. Parenting can be trying and exasperating. At those times, it is easy to do more damage than you are aware of if you aren't careful. We want to bring these messages to light so we as parents can make an internal decision, outside any emotional trigger, not to ever communicate certain messages that could scar our kids.

1. "Just Do Your Best"

Many parents think the phrase "just do your best" is a useful expression or even a wonderful thing to say to their kids—a cross between accountability and grace. But, saying this to your child is inviting him inside a riddle. It might even add unnecessary stress to his life. We believe it is not only ineffective to use this platitude, but it can be damaging. Before you pass judgment on what we are saying, and dismiss this as just semantics or an insignificant and unimportant distinction, please keep an open mind. Then decide what you think.

First, try saying the statement "Just do your best" out loud a few times. It even sounds like a riddle. Wouldn't it make more sense to pair *just* with something that has to do with being average or OK? "Just be mediocre" makes sense—just do your best doesn't. Someone's best is the absolute limit of what he can do. Saying, "just do the limit of what you can do" seems like an odd way to use the word *just*. Think about this. Best is unachievable over time, when you think about it. It requires us to always give a perfect effort.

It's a Riddle

There are three major problems with telling your child to "just do your best." First, it is an elusive, unachievable goal. When your teenager has an English paper due in a week and you tell him, "Just do your best," he will inevitably fail to do his *best*. If your son watches any TV that week, goes to a movie or high-school football game, talks on the phone, or eats junk food that makes him lethargic, he won't do his best in writing the English paper. He could have written a better paper if he hadn't done any one of those things.

In other words, when parents say "just do your best" to a child, they are really saying, "Just don't do anything that has any chance of negatively impacting your paper." You may be thinking, *That is not what I mean when I say that.* Exactly. Then don't say it at all, because that is what the child must respond to, whether she knows what you mean or not.

For brief periods in life, it is possible and perhaps a good idea to *do your best*, but those times are usually few and far between. A child doing his best on a four-hour test, doing her best at a tennis match, or doing his best in a job interview are all reasonable and perhaps helpful exceptions. All these examples encompass a short timeframe in which a best effort is reasonable and helpful.

Ultimately, kids do better if a parent's expectations are well articulated and clearly defined, not just the vague riddle of "just do your best."

The Law of Diminishing Returns

Second, *just do your best* messes with something called the *Law of Diminishing Returns*. Our kids need to be trained in understanding the Law of Diminishing Returns to work effectively in the world. But this law is in complete opposition to the maxim *just do your best*. The Law of Diminishing Returns is an innate part of our everyday thinking. When it comes to any particular endeavor, we have to intuitively understand how to find the point of diminishing returns. If we think to ourselves, *five minutes is enough time to spend on this e-mail*, we are using the Law of Diminishing Returns. If we don't implement this principle, our lives become inefficient and unbalanced.

Telling kids to "just do your best" delays their learning this important law. It would be more effective to encourage them to find the point of diminishing returns. Ask them if they know the *right* amount of time to put into a situation. If they don't know, help them with this. Mowing the lawn, emptying the dishwasher, washing the car, maybe even doing a math assignment are all things kids should learn to do good enough.

It is fine to have high expectations for our kids. It's our role as parents to encourage and instruct our children to commit to something, focus on something, or even carry out an extraordinary effort toward something. We are not advocating lowering expectations.

If your daughter has a part in the school play and is concerned about learning her lines, tell her to have Act I memorized by Saturday. Define what she needs to do in achievable steps. It is not important whether she memorized her lines by *doing her best*. It is simply important that she knows her part. Telling her to do her best gives her no roadmap to actually do what she needs to do.

In rare circumstances, it does make sense to say, "Do your best." Take the example of a gifted young musician who is auditioning to attend Julliard on a full scholarship. *Do your best* is meaningful here. But for most kids, it is usually better to have a 3.4 GPA, enjoy a social life, take pictures for the yearbook, and participate in a theater production, than it is for them to get a 3.8 GPA and live in isolation with no other interests, which is what *doing your best* would entail.

Finally, it's really hard to figure out how to do your best. Thousands of athletes are surprised to find that their game has not really improved after an intense off-season of conditioning and reducing body fat. Training year-round and repeated motion injuries (RSIs) can be the result of an athlete attempting to do his best instead of finding the point of diminishing returns. The *do your best* mindset is responsible for reduced accomplishments in many athletes. This is currently a major topic of discussion and study with sports trainers and sports psychologists. The conversation is moving to the public as the merits of cross training in different sports and taking a season off from a sport gains more support from the sports community.

TEACHING KIDS TO LIE

A third reason we are opposed to *just do your best* is that the whole dialogue around it is a breeding ground for lying and self-deception. This puts kids in a situation where they must lie to themselves to justify their efforts because they didn't do their best. They also end up lying to their parents so mom and dad can feel good about them doing their best. If the emotional economy and the vocabulary in the home support it, kids will start using that phrase without thinking. It becomes the accepted phraseology in the home. Kids learn what to say that will work for them in the family system. To diminish conflict they learn to say, "Leave me alone" or "I didn't mean to" or "She started it." They also learn that saying, "But, I did my best," gets people off their back.

In a family where the vocabulary is all about doing one's

best, it would be an unusually mature kid who could say, "I didn't do my best; however I put about as much time into that as it merited, and I think I did pretty well."

There is a price to be paid for integrating this platitude into the family system. "Just do your best" statements are likely to lead to self-deception or stress. Either the child will be dishonest about her efforts or, if the child in question is honest, she will find it stressful because she will repeatedly have to admit that she *could* have done better. Giving something your best leaves nothing out, which takes a lot of focus and self-discipline. We need to do as much as possible to reduce stress and self-lying because self-deception is at the core of low self-esteem, fear, addiction, and delusional thinking.

> *If our perceptions of ourselves are incorrect, we will probably be prone to maladjustment. We can only adjust to reality if we have an accurate perception of it. We create a major component of our own reality, and if we have an unrealistic view of ourselves, we have distorted reality.*
>
> *Addictive Thinking,*
> - Abraham J. Twerski, MD

How to Encourage Balance

Encourage balance by thinking along these lines for your child: How do I promote an understanding of working toward a goal that's reasonable for him, while helping him efficiently achieve that goal and be balanced about how much time it requires? What is an appropriate amount of pressure for him to experience as he works toward that goal?

How do you get your head around this as a parent? You need to tell your child specifically what it is you want or expect from her. It's appropriate to tell your daughter that you expect her to get at least a 3.0 GPA this semester, if that is a reasonable expectation for her. Tell your daughter you want her to play with intensity and have fun at the basketball tournament. Tell your son that you'd like him to eat nutritious food at his friend's cabin. Or, tell him you want him to be in bed by 10:00 p.m. the night before his cross-country race.

Replace the phrase "Just do your best" with tangible or balanced terms, and do not tell your child, "All we expect is your best." Your child doesn't know what that means. Nobody knows what that means.

2. "We Did That Stuff When We Were Kids!"

When parents say, "We did that stuff when we were kids," it's usually in reference to kids doing something foolish, dangerous, or illegal. If you are a parent who uses this rationalization in your parenting, you need to consider how unsound this thinking is.

This phrase is sometimes communicated to kids. More often, it is communicated in a conversation between parents and friends. Most of the time, parents use this thinking when it's related to a risky activity. But this rationalization offers no useful information when you are assessing whether or not you should allow your child to engage in dangerous, foolish, or illegal behavior. While it may be true that you did x, y, or z when you were your child's age, that fact is irrelevant to what your child is going through right now. Sometimes parents have difficulty separating what they did growing up with what their child is currently dealing with. This can be at their children's peril.

Consider this logic: A dad grew up near a small lake where he had access to a fishing boat with an old Evinrude outboard motor. On hot summer days, he and his friends would take the boat out on the lake, swim, and go tubing around the lake to cool off. Thinking back on those summer evenings, he recalls that he and his buddies never bothered wearing life jackets.

Fast-forward thirty years. This dad now has a son who is seventeen years old and the dad finds out the son just spent a weekend at some friend's cabin on a lake. All weekend they were tubing without life jackets. If the dad thinks, *well, we did that stuff when we were kids*, he is falling victim to a phenomenon known as the *narrative fallacy.* In logic, the narrative fallacy is our need to attach a story or pattern to a series of connected or disconnected facts, which serves to distort the interpretation of the facts.

The narrative of this dad's personal tubing story is altering and interfering with the accuracy of the way he is interpreting his son's story. Most of us do this. If we hear a story or remember something that happened to us, even if it's as simple as how we got over a cold, it can alter data as we process current information.

For the son, tubing without a life jacket is exactly as dangerous (or as safe) as it is. Dad's experience tubing thirty years earlier without a life jacket (and not drowning) has nothing to do with the risk his son is taking now. We don't know what the probability factor is, but the son has the exact same probability of drowning on the lake, regardless of anything his dad did thirty years ago. Dad's experience tubing thirty years earlier has no relevance in what he should decide to do about his son's weekend.

The narrative fallacy is most dangerous when the story involves danger. This would include anything a parent remembers fondly from his or her past that involved poor judgment—but a high price was not paid. These memories serve to do nothing more than to distort thinking. This thinking can be distorted in either direction—it can make something dangerous seem safer than it is, such as parents who drove while they were high as teenagers, but never experienced an accident. Or, it can make something safe feel more dangerous than it is. If thirty years earlier a dad went skiing one time and broke his leg, this dad may perceive skiing as more dangerous than statistics or logic would support.

ALLOWING SMART RISKS

The goal is not to keep our children totally safe. In fact, it is extremely dangerous to try to raise kids too safely, so we strongly endorse *smart risks*. The goal is to assess as accurately as possible the opportunity that is before your children.

Smoking weed (which increasingly may be laced with something to amp it up), drinking eighteen shots on your eighteenth birthday, driving after a drink or two, white-water rafting, sleeping around, getting a tattoo in Mexico, and yes—even skiing—are all things that are exactly as dangerous as they are.

These risks do not change because of your story. Your story can distort your judgment today with your own children. The fact that you may have engaged in some risky activities in your teen years without consequence should have no bearing at all on whether your child should engage in those activities. Remember, there is a better chance that your personal history is distorting your objectivity than it is helping your thinking today.

It may be impossible to precisely assess any risk, but we will do a better job if we are aware that our stories are often not helping our assessment. Research, discussions, and an expert opinion can be useful, but someone's story is not.

3. Those Ineffective Threats, Reminders, and Warnings

There are exceptions, but a good rule to live by is to avoid threats, reminders, and warnings while raising your kids. When parents hear this concept, they sometimes respond, "If I took away threats, reminders, and warnings I would have very little left. That is how I keep control as a parent." We think there are better options for influencing your kids.

THREATS

Threats are simply ineffective. Their use is overrated. By using threats, you are teaching your child that he doesn't really have to listen to you until the threats start coming. Typically, a boy raised in a home that uses threats will tend to play a video game long after his bedtime because he doesn't even think about closing down the game until the threats start coming. A home is not a place where someone should have to use threats to be taken seriously. For that matter, neither is school nor work. How would it feel for you as an adult to have an atmosphere of threats every day at your workplace?

Don't be fooled by the times that a threat gets you the desired behavior you were looking for. Threats may get your daughter to put her bike away. However, if we look at discipline from the perspective that it is designed to elevate a child's behavior across the board, are your threats working? Here's a simple way to find out: If your daughter puts her bike away on the day she was threatened, we could conclude that threats didn't really work, if she leaves her bike out again tomorrow. In this case, the threats did nothing to grow her up, in spite of the fact that her bike is now in the garage.

Also, many threats are unenforceable, vague, and poorly developed. Threats often teach your child that you don't know what to do or you don't mean what you say. In fact, you may actually feel a little out of control when you are expressing a threat. The classic, "or else!" reveals to your child with certainty that you have little or no idea what you are doing right then. Parents might as well say out loud, "I don't know what to do next," rather than the habitual "or else."

Finally, threats usually reveal a parent's emotional investment in the outcome. The best learning environment for your child is when the parent has no emotional stake in the issue. This dynamic isn't always possible, but when it is present, it is powerful. Parenting with no emotional stake in the issue makes it most likely that the child will learn from an event. When parents can stay emotionally detached, they improve the learning climate immensely.

Using this approach, a parent might say, "Clean the gutters and you can go out Friday night. Don't clean the gutters and I get to have you home with me. Either option is fine with me. I'd like hanging out with you this weekend anyway." This creates the best learning atmosphere at home. In the right setting, you could say something like, "You can mow the lawn Saturday and I will pay you twenty dollars. If the lawn isn't mowed by noon on Sunday I will call your cousin and pay him the twenty dollars. We don't need to talk about it again and I am fine with either choice."

We are distinguishing between threats and data in this section. Repeatedly saying to your daughter, "You better keep that phone off at night or I'm going to give it to your brother," is only a threat if there is no follow through and nothing changes as she sends texts throughout the night. However, if you calmly take the phone and give it to her brother, then that comment was data. Kids need to know the precise and accurate data or information pertaining to the consequences of their decisions. Too often statements that start with, "You better ..." are threats because nothing significant ever changes in the child's world.

REMINDERS

Does reminding your child to do things make him a better "rememberer" or a better forgetter? We often hear parents say, "I remind him and remind him and he still forgets." Of course he forgets. In a home full of parental reminders, the son knows that somebody needs to remember the dark blue jersey and he knows Mom will do that. Reminders teach our children to be forgetters.

Parents may just think about the moment and forget their job is getting their kids ready for adulthood. They just want to make sure their child doesn't miss an event or forget to take her soccer spikes to practice. But, they are missing the overall goal, which is raising a responsible, mindful, life-ready young adult. Solving the problem with constant reminders won't develop a child in this way.

Reminders also relieve the child of their personal responsibility and transfer it onto someone else. Often kids say something like this when they forget to take a make-up test or an appointment for the family photo, "It's not my fault; you didn't remind me."

Recently, a forty-six-year-old woman said that after twenty-three years of never once forgetting her husband's birthday, this year she forgot it. For years she had always remembered the day, but recently she had become accustomed to having her iPhone remind her about birthdays and had misplaced her phone the day before his birthday. It is fine to use a calendar to remember things or something like Post-It notes. The point is simply that reminders make us forgetters. If we need reminders, it should be something for which we take responsibility. We can hardly be angry with our child for forgetting a backpack if we have proven to him that it is our job to remember the backpack.

WARNINGS

There are limited situations where warnings are a good strategy. Warnings work at the airport or at a national park when we are warned about a situation we are unfamiliar with. For example, "Don't feed the bears," or "Please place all fluids in a Zip-Lock bag." Warnings work at home when the caution concerns a situation that may be new to our child.

For instance, telling a four-year-old that something is hot—or telling a sixteen-year-old that the roads are slippery—are examples of using a warning appropriately. These give new and potentially important information. A warning that conveys new information is helpful and appropriate in the family. "Be careful, they are forecasting a storm for later this afternoon" is an informational warning and is helpful. Warning also works well when someone outside the family system makes the warning. The park ranger and the airport announcements are not part of our personal family systems. Warning a neighbor kid or warning your niece may yield the precise and desired response because we are warning someone who is outside the family system.

These exceptions rarely take place in the family. This is why "don't warn" makes the list of things not to say to your children. The classic, "I'm warning you" is meaningless, impotent, unclear, and self-sustaining. If you have a twelve-year-old boy who is supposed to be off the computer by 9:00 p.m., there is nothing productive about warning him that it is 9:10. Often warnings simply pollute the atmosphere in the home, fill it with tension and words that hurt relationships. When warnings are used repeatedly in the context of a family system, they become essentially worthless.

Kids learn at an early age what the *warning quota* is for certain offenses. They learn how many warnings usually accompany "turn off your phone" and how many go with "you can't wear that top." It's almost like a softball player who knows how many balls he needs to take to get a walk. If there are five warnings to practice the violin, the child learns this and the first four warnings are meaningless and just fill the home with negative noise.

It is far more effective, especially with a challenging child, to handle things in a way that doesn't involve warnings. For instance, if the family adopted a practice where the TV was on a timer and the TV would shut off at 9:00 p.m., there would be no need to warn, remind, or threaten concerning kids watching TV too late. The house would be peaceful and the kids would just expect the TV to go off at the time it always went off. Granted, the first two weeks this plan was implemented, there might be some opposition, but soon it will work smoothly.

Of course, periodic warnings are fine and can even serve a purpose in a family. The point is that in many homes, warnings have become meaningless background noise and have long ago stopped being an asset to the family system. If you listen to the dialogue in your home and hear more than one or two warnings in an entire day—they have probably lost their usefulness.

4. Unloading on Kids

It is understandable that parenting can push some parents to the limit of their sanity like nothing else can. We have immense empathy for parents who are up pacing the floor at 3:00 a.m., wiping away tears while they repeatedly check the driveway hoping their daughter or son will come home safely. We have both been these parents. We know many others who have gone through this as well and it is terribly difficult.

In these difficult times, it is important not to forget that this child is also in pain and in danger. It is important to decide beforehand what messages you will never communicate, regardless of the situation. No matter how dark the blackness gets, don't ever tell your child he or she is unwanted. Don't slip and say what you don't mean. Don't say it even if you do mean it. No one thing is as damaging to the psyche of a child as being told he or she is or was unwanted.

Extreme comments sound like this:

- "I wish you were never born."
- "I regret that we adopted you."
- "I can't wait for you to leave home."
- "You were a huge mistake. We should have stopped at two children."
- "You have brought pain into my life since you were born."
- "Because you were born my life was ruined."

Milder versions of the same comments are:

- "Next year you will be out of here and we won't have to deal with you."
- "You have always been more difficult than your brother, even when you were little."
- "Maybe you'll have a child like you someday and then you'll know what it's like."

You may be mildly aghast to think that any conscientious parent would ever say those things. Yet they are said all the time. We hear about it in our practices. It may happen on a dark and scary night when your job is particularly difficult, when that youngest child is seventeen and you have been parenting for twenty-nine years and you are exhausted, or when you feel sorry for yourself. We can empathize with the situation. Just work really hard to not ever say those words to your child, even if that is how you feel.

If you have already said those words to your child, it is likely that you need to get more support. It may be appropriate for you to go to your child and say, "Last spring, when things were really rough between us, I said some things I never should have said. It would have been easy for you to think that you have only brought sadness to me. That is not true and that was my fear speaking. That may even be part of why we are not getting along right now. You are very precious to me." It is never too late to try to reconcile a wrong. Though it may take a while, both sides benefit from an apology.

There are numerous ways to express your feelings in a situation without it being blatant rejection.

You can say things like:

- "I never thought we would be down this road together."
- "With your behavior, you are choosing to not live here anymore."
- "I love you, but I hate seeing you this way."
- "I wish you could know how much I love you. I know that it doesn't show when I get this angry at your lies."

We believe in honest and open parenting. Just be careful on this issue; it can be so damaging. Harsh rejection from a parent can wound a child's soul. Some parents reading this book may remember some of these things said to them. They will know firsthand what a hurdle that is to get over.

The GIST of It

- Avoid saying, "Just do your best." It usually works better to tell him what you expect. More power to him if he can do what you expect without it being his best.

- Be careful not to say anything so hurtful that you can never take it back.

- Threats, reminders, and warnings are not helpful.

- Your own childhood stories do not really help with decisions and perspectives today. Our stories are more about probability than they are about evidence.

- Be extra careful what you say to your child when you are hurt, scared, angry, or confused.

Chapter Nineteen:
The Black Hole of Technology

The world has witnessed an exponential explosion of technology over the last twenty years. Most of us have watched this not knowing how to handle it in terms of our children's well-being. Even preschoolers are now immersed in technology.

One of the hardest parts of parenting in the millennial age is what to do about technology. It is here to stay ... that's a fact. Whether we like it or not, it has become a huge part of all our lives. No doubt, many technological advances have dramatically changed our lives for the better (medicine, traffic control, scheduling, paying bills, efficient communication, research, etc.). What we address in this chapter focuses on "communication and entertainment" technologies and their impact on the lives of our children and, ultimately, on our society.

Our caution about technology and media falls into four main areas of concern: 1) The sheer volume of time spent on media, 2) The content of the media, 3) The interruptions to focus and living life that it causes, and 4) The stressful and unnatural situations it can so easily put our children in.

Technology consumes more time in the days of our children than anything else—except sleep (and, for an increasing number, sleep is #2). This increasing time spent on non- educational technologies doesn't make kids' lives any easier, just more overloaded and stress-filled. Once thought to make our lives more efficient, communication and entertainment technologies have had the opposite effect on most young people.

This is an area of parenting that has been brewing over these last years and has received little attention until recently. Parents now have an entire new layer to deal with, as compared to one generation ago. Unfortunately, many parents have just let it all happen, confused and uncertain what to do. Unfortunately, many parents have found themselves caught up in unregulated screen time.

One of our primary motives in writing this book is to address the stress that our clients and patients exhibit. Technology can be one of the biggest factors increasing stress in children. Our world has come to believe (or has been misled to believe) that all technology is progress and progress is good. We don't believe technology is necessarily synonymous with progress. The progress the world calls real is actually *presumed progress*. The challenge comes in how we must balance it and teach our kids to do the same.

Common Sense Media reported in 2015 that kids between 8 and 12 years old were spending, on average, 41 hours a week on media. Kids 13 to 18 years old were spending over 60 hours on media per week. And this number excludes time spent on media for school and homework. That may sound almost unbelievable, but when you combine the multitasking of social media interaction, texting, TV, and video gaming that take place on the bus, in the bedroom, at school, in the car, waiting for a ride, or hanging with friends, it certainly becomes a very believable number. As most kids are only awake for 15 or 16 hours per day, this means that somewhere between 71 and 76 percent of their day is spent living in the digital world. You don't have to look far to see examples in children's lives. You don't have to look far to see it in adults.

The same study estimates that teenage boys average 56 minutes a day on video games. An innumerable number of boys are playing over 4 hours a days. Video gaming, especially for boys and young men, is linked with academic failure, behavioral irritability, and the disappearance of motivation.

Texting, tweeting, and snapchat are the primary modes of communication of young people, bypassing direct face to face conversation where facial expression, inflection, social skills and emotions are in play. Texting interferes with classroom teaching and the ability for our kids to concentrate amidst unending interruptions. At an average of 3,400 texts per month, the typical teen has a lot to respond to, the majority of which is trivial. We don't believe this is the best way to communicate.

Technology has become a big factor contributing to overload for families and kids. If your children are young, don't be fooled into thinking this doesn't yet apply to your household. Even parents of toddlers need to be aware. This may feel pretty dark to many parents, but awareness can be the first step in understanding and, ultimately, balance with this technology. Now, let's unpack some of our concerns about the common issues relating to technology we are currently seeing in our offices.

1. Smartphones

Smartphones are an incredible technological phenomenon. Just a few years ago it would have been hard to imagine having a personal computer, cell phone, digital camera, portable gaming device, home calendar, MP3 player, flashlight, alarm clock, and GPS device that all fits in your pocket. But there is a price to pay for these amazing phones, and it's not just the monthly data plan cost.

The biggest question parents may not ask before getting a smartphone for their child is this: Is my child ready for the responsibility of a smartphone? Is it wise for my child to have the Internet at his fingertips twenty-four hours a day? If the child is not ready, a smartphone will invariably bring more overload into his life. Smartphones are marketed to teens because they are the fastest growing demographic of users.

If parents take time to look at the positives and negatives of smartphones, they might pause before getting that iPhone or android for their thirteen-year-old. Using smartphones to cheat on tests at school is epidemic.

Another major negative to cell phone use in teenagers has to do with distracted driving (we should include adults in this issue as well). In 2013, 3,154 people were killed and an estimated additional 424,000 were injured in motor vehicle crashes involving distracted drivers. For teens, 15 percent of distracted drivers were distracted by cell phones.

2. Video Gaming

Video gaming started out relatively innocuously with games such as *Pong, Pac-Man, Centipede,* and *Asteroids.* Those first generation games weren't very realistic or complex. By contrast, many of today's games have content and language that is graphically violent and sexualized. The objectives have dramatically changed and now include theft, murder, and acting out sexual fantasies. Instead of playing a video game together with a friend, kids now play video games online with dozens and sometimes hundreds of total strangers. Some of these fellow-gamers are predators.

- Seventy-two percent of Americans ages six to forty-four play a screen-based game an average of eighteen hours per week.

- Four percent of Americans are "extreme gamers," playing at least fifty hours per week.

- Some eight and a half percent of Americans ages eight to eighteen are clinically addicted to gaming with a four to one ratio of boys to girls.

- South Korea and China have opened several hundred treatment centers for video gaming addiction.

Research is now leading to more conclusive evidence of what can happen in the brains of gamers. The consequences of this even have medical evidence. The area of the brain responsible for translating motivation into action is called the *nucleus accumbens* (NA), also known as one of the brain's pleasure centers. It is considered an important area involved with addiction and can be "turned on" by several chemicals like cocaine, narcotics, and alcohol as well as certain activities like sex, eating, and video gaming. Video games are intentionally designed to activate this part of the brain. Many games start out free, then the fees and the costs come in after the child is hooked.

Another related area of the brain, the *dorsal prefrontal cortex* (DLPFC), is important in helping us find a target for a particular drive we have and relate it to the context of our world. The DLPFC essentially balances the NA, helping us put our motivations into an action that is appropriately targeted. Gaming has been shown to decrease the oxygenation of the DLPFC. What does that tell us? These games stimulate our brain's pleasure center with little effort, while hindering our ability to relate it (the VG achievement) to anything contextually substantial. The human brain is fooled into feeling that something was achieved, yet with little context in the real world. We believe this results in thinking that there is more reward in entertainment (the video game) than in accomplishing something of value. Essentially, these games offer a sense of accomplishment without any actual accomplishment.

The addictive nature of video games is present regardless of the content of the video game. Whether it's benign games, such as preschool games and building games, or violent games, the result for many kids is the same. Three-year-olds can become addicted just like thirteen-year-olds and twenty-three-year-olds. We see many patients whose school achievement plummets. We see preschoolers whose ability to relate with family and friends has regressed. Whatever the age, kids begin the process of falling behind.

Kids who play video games extensively carry with them a very unique stress. They are experts at something that doesn't really exist. They can play football on a screen really well, but they have never played the sport on a field. The same goes for *League of Legends* and *World of Warcraft* players who are battle experts in a world that doesn't exist. They carry with them the awareness that they are elite in a virtual world, but less accomplished in the real world.

Video gaming also contributes to overload for the same reason as social networking—it takes time. The medical and psychiatric communities are currently discussing a possible new diagnostic code for video game addiction. It's a real problem.

3. Social Networking

Social networking sites like Facebook and Instagram consume hours a day for many teens and tweens, as well as adults. Parents see the rapidly addictive properties of these types of sites. When their child starts it, they can't stop. Many have to check their Facebook page wherever they are—whether it's on vacation, at Grandma's house, or in the school library. The goal is to meet some of their needs by using a virtual identity, a virtual community, or virtual adventure. Sometimes this is easier than putting up with the real world and all its complexities and challenges. Perhaps they just want an escape. Maybe they are afraid of being left out from the inner circle. Whatever the motive, much of their childhood can be spent managing and worrying about the impressions they are making on other kids.

While the social media of choice is changing all the time, all social networking has given people the ability to connect with strangers they'll never meet and predators they'll hopefully never meet. Social networking has created a world in which people can take on pseudo identities and superficially connect with people, all the while wasting hours and missing out on real life. Granted, when used appropriately, these sites can connect friends and family more closely than was possible in the past. However, it can become an alternate identity if we aren't careful. This is not what socializing is about. Kids need to believe that they can't create their identity on a keyboard.

Social networking sites have become one of the most "evaluated" parts of a person's identity. Those applying for a job, a scholarship, a graduate program, a ministerial position, or dental school should be aware of this. High school students who participate in sports need to know that a picture of them at a party could end their high school sports careers.

For many, social networking sites tend to be a representation of a child's false self: that person they feel they need to portray to the rest of the world. It's the person who looks good in the selected pictures, the person who always is having fun, and the person who is surrounded by friends.

From a parenting perspective, seventy-six percent of parents help their teen set up a social networking site, yet only eighteen percent of the parents are "friends" with their child. Twelve percent of teens spend more than three hours per day on Facebook/Instigram/Snapchat counting the time it's running as a background.

According to a 2015 study by the Pew Research Center, about 92% of teens report going online daily to social network — including 24% who say they go online "almost constantly". Many teens set up dummy Facebook sites, or they use settings to limit what they share with their parents. So the parent doesn't see the whole picture.

Today, the most popular growing form of social networking for children and teens is Twitter. Tweeting is concerning because of its inherent ability to spin a message out of control. A twitter post can fly through a school in just minutes. Imagine that a shy, immature teen tweets to a few friends something foolish about a classmate, a compromising photo of a friend, or a derogatory comment about a chemistry teacher. In seconds, that post can be received, and in a minute, it can be re-tweeted to another group of followers, who could then re-tweet it to their followers. A brief, thoughtless message or photo could reach 400 kids and adults in a community in five minutes. This presents a new type of risk for our kids. This is a new level of scope and speed whereby humiliation, embarrassment, or damage can be inflicted in an irretrievable way. Again, nothing is private and nothing is safe in a "Twitter world."

As popular as Twitter has become, it is still too early to grasp all of the implications of this phenomenon. Some experts have predicted that in the end, Twitter will be the most destructive form of social networking of all. Besides time spent reading the tweets from people they follow, kids also have to figure out what to "properly" tweet in response. #CRAZY.

4. Cyber-Bullying

Cyber-bullying is any targeted threat of offensive behavior done over the Internet or cell phones. It includes hurtful messages, rumors, false identity, slander, incriminating or embarrassing photos, or hacking. According to the Cyberbullying Research Center, some eighty-eight percent of teens have witnessed another person cyber-bullying a peer. That is most of our kids. Serious emotional consequences have resulted, including depression and suicidal thoughts and attempts, some successful. Bullying can be mild or severe. The mildest form of bullying might be to tease someone about what neighborhood they live in or what jacket they're wearing. The severest form of bullying might be to make false claims or spread slanderous photos that cut into the heart of a teen's identity.

Most states now have laws that address bullying in schools. Schools, colleges, and universities that are federally funded have an obligation to resolve the harassment. If the situation is not resolved at the school level, the U.S. Department of Education's Office for Civil Rights and the U.S. Department of Justice's Civil

Rights Division can be called in to help. This is serious stuff.

One aspect of cyber-bullying that makes it particularly complex is that nearly half of all kids that are bullies are also concurrently being bullied. Let's translate that this way: Nearly half the kids we need to protect our children from, also need to be protected. It becomes hard to know where our anger should be directed.

Unfortunately, cyber-bullying is an offense experienced by far too many children and teenagers. Adults must begin to be more involved in the virtual lives of their children and intervene when cyber-bullying takes place. Whether protecting your child from this or preventing your child from doing it, parents need to step up to ensure the right thing is being done. We believe parents have every right to oversee and monitor their child's online activities, especially where there is concern over their child's wellbeing. The costs are too high not to do so.

5. Sexting

Sexting is the sending and receiving of sexually explicit pictures and text messages. According to the government's Child Exploitation and Online Protection Centre, sexting is increasingly becoming normalized among teenagers, who often don't realize they may be acting illegally and could face police action. This is most commonly seen in the middle school and early high school age. An estimated twenty percent of thirteen- to nineteen-year-olds have texted explicit photos of themselves; thirty-nine percent have posted sexually suggestive messages.

Where these pictures go cannot be controlled once the child hits 'send'. Many innocent and naive kids have had an image, meant just for a few friends, sent all over a school or community. Sometimes images are distributed far beyond their community. One girl's picture was being viewed by soldiers serving in

Afghanistan, while in another serious case, a 17-year-old boy was jailed for 12 months after demanding that two 14-year-olds send him indecent images of themselves on Snapchat.

Unfortunately, kids do not think about the potential for dire consequences. Digital messages can be distributed to others very easily and en masse. Kids often forget that things they send may be forwarded to others. Once these messages are "out there" they cannot be retrieved. It is almost impossible to take back things posted on the Internet, e-mail, or sent via text. Surprisingly, really good kids get sucked into this behavior. It is the parent's responsibility to intervene if a child is using his or her phone in this way. There are laws against sending nude or partially nude photos from a cellphone. Some teens have been charged with felonies for child porn distribution. Our children need this knowledge to help them make the smart decisions with these risks all around them.

6. Internet Pornography

Online pornography sites are often just a few clicks away. More kids are exposed to porn at a younger age and with a broader exposure than ever before. By their teen years, most girls and boys have viewed at least some form of online pornography, including intercourse (heterosexual and homosexual), group sex, and bestiality. This can be hard to imagine as a parent.

Over the past decade, as porn desensitization took place in the minds and culture of our youth, adult complacency accompanied it. Parents need to know the results of this exposure at such a young age. A staggering thirteen percent of all Internet searches are for pornography. Multiple studies have shown a close association between frequent exposure to explicit sexual material and permissive attitudes about sexual behaviors such as having multiple partners, one-night stands, casual sex with friends, and hooking up.

Will our children ever be able to erase those images of hardcore porn in their young brains? Will our sons or daughters take those images with them to their future relationships? Will those images affect their relationship with a spouse? Will they always compare their sexual performance by what they saw online when they were fourteen? We contend these images are damaging to young brains. Young brains have no way to process these harsh images.

A Parent's Role

What we see in our clinical practices is concerning. We see family after family with no reasonable limits or boundaries for their children's use of technology. It's as if they think a child who can play *Call of Duty* really well will somehow be able to transfer that skill to a job in computer engineering. That's a myth. In fact, out of the eight and a half hours a day that a child is "plugged in", a 2015 TIME magazine article estimated that teens, on average, spend less than nine minutes a day doing anything creative at all related with their digital world.

We suggest that parents regularly disconnect their kids and allow them to take a break from technology, sometimes for extended periods of time. We recommend that families completely disconnect when they go on vacation, and leave their children's cell phones, laptops, and gaming devices home. The feedback we have received from families who have done this is always the same: the family experience turned out to be fantastic. It doesn't mean there wasn't resistance, because there usually was. We tell parents not to be fooled by the first two days of your *disconnected* vacation. Although this idea will be unpopular, give it a try. You'll like what you see.

TECHNOLOGY IS NOT A RIGHT, IT'S A PRIVILEGE

We also suggest that parents make sure their kids are aware of who owns the Internet connection. Today's child *should not* be in control of, or given any autonomy over the household's Internet connections. When they are allowed to have that kind of control over their parents and families, the result is invariably bad. Many parents don't feel like they can limit this "right of technology" their child believes he or she should have. Technology is not a *right*; it is a privilege.

Technology disputes are one of the most common areas of difficulty for parents, and needlessly so. The answer to this dilemma for parents is ridiculously easy, yet many don't employ their parental authority to deal with the issue at the beginning. Some parents don't want to establish restrictions because it is too inconvenient for them or the rest of the family. Some don't want to think about restrictions because they're afraid of conflict. Many parents don't utilize this great source of power: the privilege to allow use of technology in the home. They give it away to their child.

Parents need to be creative, clever, and intentional. Putting the home Wi-Fi on a timer is a simple example. Requiring that cell phones be turned in before bed is reasonable and recommended. Removing video game or TV power cords when your kid is at school is easy. Turning off the circuit breaker to the family room is a thirty-second process. It's OK to say to your kid, "I'm going to figure out a way to shut you down." If he responds, "I'll figure out how to turn it back on," at least he's learning how to solve problems. Tell your child the screen time and technology use will depend on him keeping a healthy balance to his life.

The bottom line is that the parent must lead the way for *balance* in their child's life as it relates to using technology. This includes the parents not being overly dependent (or even addicted) to their own sources of technology.

INVISIBLE CONSEQUENCES

There are many invisible consequences of excess technology that many parents don't consider. We are now seeing these emerge in large numbers of young adults. First, so much of conversational learning comes from the give and take of dialogue with another person. As children grow up to be young adults, those who over-rely on technology to communicate seem to be losing the art and skill of conversation. Business owners hire college graduates who have difficulty relating in conversation. We believe it's because they have grown up relating to others through computers and phones, and not face-to-face.

Second, the ability to work with others in a group is becoming a lost skill in our kids. Their time spent on technology has neutralized their learning to work with others. Growing up in today's world, they spend much less time in groups, interacting with other people for a common goal, negotiating, developing a group-think, and compromising. Twenty-five years ago these were skills learned in the backyards of every neighborhood by kids playing together. These same skills now seem to be disappearing. The average person's time on the Internet has doubled in the past five years according to ZenithOptimedia. They tell us we will soon find even more time in the day to take in media—half of our waking life is apparently not enough.

A third issue that technology is hindering is the ability of young adults to solve problems on their own. A dependency on technology has affected so much of what used to be very expected skills. For example, many young adults don't know how to read a map. They have never had to read a map because they can enter an address on a screen and it will tell them where to go. In the real world, businessmen and women notice that recent graduates struggle with how to begin solving problems in the workplace. If they can't Google it, they are stymied. Without a computer helping them, they just don't know what to do.

Youth treatment programs see amazing growth in kids simply by taking them away from electronics and forcing them to narrow their focus to living in the real world, using problem- solving skills in real life with no access to outside stressors or solutions. We have had experience on youth and humanitarian trips where kids are not allowed access to social media for a week or two. The transformation is incredible. Many who learned to unplug during those experiences continue unplugging occasionally after they return to their "normal" lives because it was so refreshing.

THE NEWEST HUMAN REFLEX

Technology has not only changed how we function, but also how we think. In the decade after the mobile Internet became part of our daily lives, we started to see people actually behave and think differently than in the past. There are many life situations we face that are considered challenges. People face these challenges every day in their cars, in shops, at work, on street corners, and in schools. Some of these challenges are present in a clinical setting in our offices. Fifteen years ago, these same challenges would have resulted in a person's face taking on a contemplative thoughtful look. Today, we see these same challenges managed with a quick, almost reflexive, move toward a smartphone.

I need to think has, in part, been replaced with, *I need to search*. Our brain's ways of functioning seem to be changing. If "use it or lose it" is true, we wonder if we will eventually have entire thought processes no longer in use. Turning to a smartphone for help isn't totally new, but the mechanical reaction to search, before there has been even the beginning of a thought, is new. This change is apparent when someone is trying to remember an address or route to somewhere they have been before. Before technology, thinking and remembering were our first impulses. Today it's searching on a smartphone

Thinking and remembering have been replaced by searching.

Our entire culture is looking down more and looking up less. This reflex can be seen in adults and children alike. However, adults of middle age and beyond have experienced reflective thought, contemplation, and stillness in earlier stages of their lives as part of their growing up years. Our concern is how technology will affect those contemplative capacities in young brains, especially brains that will never have those experiences to any great extent.

Think about it this way: because of their earlier life-experience without technology, a forty-five-year-old on a hunting trip up north who is in an area with no reception will be able to handle being disconnected for a day better than a twelve-year-old who is disconnected from his electronic world for twelve hours. We as parents need to make sure our children are being offered reprieves from technology so their brains are able to develop the capacity to reflect.

The human body adapts quickly to changes in our lifestyles. It likely won't take ten generations, as some once thought, for our brains to function differently than before. If this trend continues, we may actually suppress crucial aspects of executive brain function and lose those abilities altogether. Information that we gain through a search is still information, but it underutilizes thinking, remembering, and visualizing, all qualities that have always been essential to human life. If we lose something fundamental to our humanity and our growth, we may not know it until it is too late.

Multitasking Severely Limits our Thinking

One outcome of the availability of technology is the increased prevalence of and even admiration for multitasking. Many have come to believe that multitasking increases efficiency in the workplace. Science argues against this belief. Research has shown that multitasking takes a toll on productivity and can actually impair cognitive ability. The late Clifford Nass, a Stanford professor whose pioneering research into how humans interact with technology, calls recent research results as nothing less than "a damning indictment" of multitasking's effects, summarizing the multitaskers' condition as, "They look where they shouldn't, and their memory is all sloppy." Nass also found that high multitaskers have more social problems than low-multitasking peers.

We also know that when we are interrupted, it takes a long

time to fully return to the original task. Research has determined it takes twenty-five minutes for someone to re-engage with a task following an interruption. Additionally, the usual frequency of interruptions in an office setting is every eleven minutes. Just imagine what interruptions do to worker efficiency.

> *The research is almost unanimous, which is very rare in social science, and it says that people who chronically multitask show an enormous range of deficits. They're basically terrible at all sorts of cognitive tasks.*
>
> 2013 MPR Interview
> - Clifford Nass

But what are the effects of multitasking and interruptions on the quality of work someone does? Information technology professor Alessandro Acquisti and psychologist Eyal Peer from Carnegie Mellon University studied the effect of interruptions on brainpower. Compared to the control group who experienced no interruptions, study groups that were interrupted, or told they "might be interrupted" at any time, both answered questions correctly twenty percent less often than the control group.

So how does this relate to our kids? Imagine a tenth grade girl trying to do an hour of math homework getting interrupted by twenty-seven texts during that hour. Multitasking is not a friend of mental health. It may be admired and encouraged in certain settings, but it has no positive impact on mental well-being. Multitasking is also a huge contributor to stress and poor attention. We wonder whether the constant interruption of technology may be a contributor to symptoms of ADD.

Kids will argue that the phone doesn't distract them. The

data says otherwise. Of the over six billion text messages sent each day in our country, text messages are read, on average, in under five seconds from when they arrive, with 90% of all text messages read in under three minutes. This means that an enormous amount of time is spent anticipating or waiting for a text. This is time that our kids are not completely focused on what they are doing.

Communication and entertainment technologies are realities and are here to stay. It is incumbent on parents to place healthy boundaries around their use to assure our kids' appropriate development. The way we see many children using technology won't contribute to their success, maturity, or enhance their relationships. Only when parents understand this and retake ownership of technology, will this exponential trend start to slow down. It will take a concerted effort by a large percentage of parents for technology to loosen its tight grip on our children.

The GIST of It

- Although there are some positives to communication and entertainment technology, for the most part, it is not helping our kids grow up.

- The dangerous aspects of technology continue to worsen while the involvement of parents continues to diminish. This trend needs to reverse.

- Most kids grow up today seeing and reading things on the Internet and on their phones that no reasonable parent would ever want them to see or read. This is happening at younger and younger ages and is having a consequence.

- Contrary to what children may argue, parents ultimately have control over the technology in their lives. When kids understand this from a young age, many problems can be avoided.

- The invisible consequences of technology are seen in interpersonal relationships..

- The way your family lives with communication technology is a choice. You don't need to conform to what the culture tells you.

CHAPTER TWENTY:
OVERLOADED

Jessie's Story

Jessie was a cute nine-year-old girl who seemed to have a lot going for her. Not only was school easy for her, she seemed to excel at almost everything she tried. Her parents saw in her a lot of potential in sports, music, and academics. Because they had the resources, limiting her choices was not an issue.

By the fourth grade Jessie seemed to have a passion for gymnastics. She had started in kindergarten with a tumbling class. The instructors saw her ability and convinced her parents to increase her time at the club. She began working with more advanced older girls, received coaching from top instructors, and participated on an elite competitive team. Jessie was winning local and regional competitions, but she wasn't elite. What started as a couple of hours one evening a week became eighteen to twenty hours a week of practices and competitions, not including the driving and family time that was being sacrificed. The expense was tolerable to her parents because Jessie appeared to enjoy the positive feedback from those in the gymnastics circle.

The intensity of competition increased accordingly as she grew older. To continue the success that was expected, and accommodate the higher demands of her gymnastics team and coaches, Jessie had less time to spend with friends. When injuries related to overuse became her experience, the additional time spent at the physical therapist and chiropractor started to burden her and the whole family. Jessie appeared depressed all the time, started losing her appetite, and lost a significant amount of weight. She was brought in to her doctor for evaluation of weight loss and depressed mood.

During the visit, Jessie's parents told the doctor all of their daughter's symptoms including decreased appetite, irritability, weight loss, back pain, and daily vague abdominal pain. In addition, her parents related how she excelled in gymnastics. When the doctor expressed concern about the intensity of Jessie's gymnastics schedule, her dad reminded the physician that Jessie had great potential as a gymnast and might even have a shot at the Olympics.

The doctor asked Jessie how much she liked gymnastics, since it sounded like she was very good at it. Jessie started to cry. By the end of the appointment, Jessie opened up to her doctor, telling her and her parents, "I hate gymnastics. I don't have any time to have any friends, watch TV, or be with my brother and sisters. Maybe I'm good at it, but I don't want to do it anymore."

Jessie was the victim of overload. Too much of a good thing is usually not a good thing.

Too Much on the Docket

Many children are living life out of balance. Pressure is put on children to be involved, excel, and succeed in high-profile activities. But, learning things that matter most isn't even on the back burner in their lives. They are trying to fit all the items on their schedules into time that doesn't exist. Opportunities for our children today far exceed what was available in the past, but this may not be progress or a good thing. Parents feel intense pressure to sign up their kids for all that is available to them. They are afraid their children will somehow be deprived and fall behind their peers. Worse yet, they fear their children will fall behind in this mythical thing we call *potential*.

When they do conform to cultural messages and allow them to "do it all" they are left with the paradox of tired, exhausted, and depressed children who have less meaningful interpersonal time with friends and family and miss out on a well-balanced childhood.

> *Wrongheaded ideas have a nasty habit of catching on more quickly than correct ideas. The belief that earlier is better in relation to early childhood is one such wrong idea that seems to have caught on, and it is difficult to combat. With respect to sports, there is no reliable evidence that starting children early in an individual or team sport gives them a lasting advantage or edge.*
>
> *The Hurried Child – Growing Up Too Fast Too Soon*
> - David Elkind

Parents allow their child to become overloaded and overscheduled for many reasons. It may be guilt, conforming to a cultural message that tells them they must, a desire for their child to experience a goal and team camaraderie, or something they themselves missed out on as a child. We can understand all of these motivations. Some are even valid.

Kids who develop an early desire to excel in a single-focused endeavor (sport, drama, music) run the risk of becoming isolated from the world around them, a world they ought to be experiencing. They may miss just hanging with kids their age, learning to participate in the family's chore schedule, and a sense of balance and boundaries, which are all very important. Nothing is more important for a child than developing balance and boundaries in his or her life. *Isolation excellence* (being very skilled in a narrow area) makes balance very hard to achieve.

With all of the choices available, parents need to help their children develop the skill to decide and choose what is reasonable and right for them in the context of their life, their abilities, and their motivation. This important life skill is absent in many teens today because they've never been taught to choose one thing over another. Additionally, many kids don't even think they should have to choose. They grow up thinking they are the center of the universe or that they must stay ultra-busy to keep up with the expectations of their parents and their worlds. If their desire to be involved isn't part of the equation, kids will grow up without passion to excel. They may even find it difficult to discover what is their calling in life.

> **Parents need to help their children choose what is reasonable and right for them in the context of their lives, their abilities, and their motivation.**

If you felt uncomfortable reading these words, ask yourself, "Do I enjoy having my family live a frantic one-activity-to-the-next life with little downtime?" Do you ever feel trapped in an overloaded life or feel like you're pushing your kids and your family past their thresholds of involvement, and wonder, *Is this the way life has to be for our family?*

DECISIONS AND DOMINOS

We all make decisions every day about what we eat, when we go to sleep, and what we wear. We take into consideration what's healthy or not, how tired we might be, and what the weather is going to be when we make those decisions. When it comes to commitments for our children, however, we may spend little or no time deciding which activity is right for them at their particular stage in life or ability. We just sign them up. The end result is an example of unintended parenting and our children end up with less time for creativity, downtime, and reflection.

Registering a son for travel basketball has significant

obligations for him *and* the family. Will he have time to keep up academically or will his grades take a hit? He may have three nights of practice per week and tournaments thirteen of the next fifteen weekends. This will mean lots of travel costs, some overnight hotel expenses, and time coordinating with other parents. Does the family's financial situation allow for this or will it just create more stress? There is the impact on the other children as well. Will they have access to a parent to help them with homework on the weekends? Will they get tired of being in the car driving to the next tournament while missing time with their friends? A single decision can have a domino effect on the whole family.

If a child or teen wants to add a significant commitment to his life and schedule, his parents need to teach him to give something up. There simply is not enough time to do it all. Otherwise, he will soon be in a *commitment debt* that will be stressful and exhausting. Yet how many parents integrate this type of life lesson into the training of their children? It's better if Billy quits Scouts if he's going to play travel basketball. If Tony is going to be part of the children's theater this year, he should not take three advanced placement classes. Maggie's commitment to the dance line team means she needs to cut back her work hours from twenty hours a week to eight.

FAMILY MEETING GUIDELINES

A family meeting is a great tool to use when a family decision is being made that affects everyone such as family vacations, holidays, or a sports commitment. If Billy decides to be on an AAU travel basketball team that involves thirteen tournaments over the course of the winter, it will certainly involve everyone in the family in one way or another.

There are some important guidelines for a family meeting. First, remember that a family is *not* a democracy. In the same way that school and work are not democracies, neither are families. The most votes don't get to decide. Everyone in the family deserves to be heard and respected, but everyone's vote does not count equally. You are the parents.

You may want to call a short meeting and say, "Billy has a chance to play AAU basketball this winter and if he does that, it will be a big investment by all of us. It means that mom or dad will be gone part of ten to thirteen weekends. It might mean that you kids will come along to some of the tournaments, too. This will impact all of us, so we want to hear everyone's opinion before *we* make this decision. Does anyone have any questions before we discuss this opportunity?"

If a child doesn't want to be at a family meeting it is usually best to leave them out and go ahead with the meeting. She may say, "I don't care what we do for our stupid family vacation," and walk away. Just tell her, "That's fine. Whoever is at the table will help make the decision." Then say, "I wish you would stay, but it's fine if you want to leave." Everyone who remains should be listened to respectfully and thanked for their contribution to the collective process of deciding. Then, with all this data, parents should decide what is best for the individuals involved.

We hear a lot of defensiveness and rationalization about this issue: If my daughter isn't at that gymnastic club, she'll never be on the elite squad, or if my son isn't in travel baseball, he'll never make varsity in high school. If your child has significant ability in an area, there will be pressure to do that activity year round. Parents need to be ready for that pressure, sometimes when a child is quite young. If your child is average, parents may feel a need to give them extra help through costly camps, private coaching, or strength training programs.

We see many gymnasts and hockey players burning out by tenth grade. Parents need to admit when they have a child with average ability. Some children truly are gifted, but most aren't. It's OK if your child is an average or below average athlete. Help him understand this and then find something else he can invest his time in.

LIVING THROUGH YOUR CHILD

Some parents live through their children. You can read all about them in the holiday letters you receive every year. This manifests in several ways. They may push their kids too hard and sacrifice too much for their kids. Whether they are escaping their own issues and relationships for their kids or just conforming to cultural expectations, the result is out-of-balance children and out-of-balance families.

Does Connor even like playing baseball? Have his parents ever asked? Does Evelyn have natural singing ability? Have her parents looked at that realistically? Think of all the children who feel like they must continue participating in sports, piano lessons, scouts, jazz band, dance-line, babysitting, a part-time job, youth group, girlfriends and boyfriends, and many other activities just because of pressure from their parents or other adults in their lives.

All are potentially good things, but if your child doesn't have any idea why he or she is doing something, you are missing an important aspect of parenting. You, as a family need to decide these things. You can't ask other overloaded parents what to do in your situation because the cultural baseline has such a pull on them.

Don't miss the opportunity to help your children understand what they're good at and to assist them in developing a passion for something. Parents are given signs of passion or a lack of passion from their children all the time. Tiger Woods was hitting golf balls by age three, not because his parents forced him to, but because he had clear passion to do so. He hit golf balls for hours when he was young. Put a golf club in the hands of a kid who has passion for golf, and he will hit golf balls over and over and over.

> *The superficiality of the American is the result of his hustling. It needs leisure to think things out; it needs leisure to mature. People in a hurry cannot think, cannot grow, nor can they decay. They are preserved in a state of perpetual puerility.*
>
> *The Passionate State of Mind,*
> - Eric Hoffer

A WORD ABOUT SLEEP

A high percentage of children growing up today are significantly sleep deprived, especially those kids who are overcommitted. Although we all can function on too little sleep for a while, it eventually catches up. Sleep deprivation affects our immune systems, making us more susceptible to a variety of community-acquired infections. Sleep deprivation can affect our moods, causing us to feel depressed, anxious, or irritable. Sleep deprivation negatively affects our attention, memory, and learning.

Current estimates have over ninety percent of U.S. teens not getting enough sleep. Some of it is schedule-related (too many commitments), and some of it is a consequence of the constant interruptions they live with (technology). Just know that most of this is self-inflicted.

There are other children who don't have enough going on in their lives. They may spend an inordinate amount of time sleeping their lives away, mainly out of boredom. They may act and behave as if they're depressed, sleeping when they come home from school until dinner, or well into the afternoons on weekends. Some may be depressed, but many are simply bored. These kids need parents who strongly mandate them to become involved in something. It doesn't need to be a sport or academic endeavor. It could be a volunteer opportunity at an animal shelter, or a part-time job. It really doesn't matter. It just needs to be something other than sleeping too much.

Parents should have the goal of teaching their children the valuable life skill of balancing their commitments. Balance, evaluating your margin for adding a commitment, and setting boundaries are very important things all kids needs to learn, especially those who are high achievers and enjoy being involved in many things at one time.

The GIST of It

- Before committing a child to any sport or extracurricular activity, parents need to evaluate the child's ability, passion, and existing schedule, as well as the impact of that commitment on the family's schedule and finances.

- The increasing time and financial commitment of youth sports can bring great joy to families or put unnecessary burdens on families.

- Be aware of the "domino effect" in making the right decision for a child and family. It's not simply an issue of Emily in gymnastics but how the decision impacts the parents and rest of the family.

- Be cognizant of passion when you see it in your child. Help develop it in a way that keeps the child in balance. Be aware of signs your child is not passionate and help him move on to something else.

The final two chapters, Learned Helplessness and The Impact of Stress, are more technical in content. Some may find these topics very interesting and others may find them difficult to understand and apply. We invite you to read on knowing that these chapters may not be easy, but we still believe they are very important – even essential for parents of children who have stopped engaging in life.

- TJ, MA

CHAPTER TWENTY-ONE:
LEARNED HELPLESSNESS

The American Psychological Association calls learned helplessness the "landmark theory of the century." If you have a happy, socially well-adjusted, achieving child, this chapter may not make sense to you. We still think it is important and may apply to a child you know. If you have a child who has quit on life, is withdrawn or shut down, this chapter may be the first words that help you understand him or her.

Kids who have learned to be helpless aren't bad kids and they aren't lazy. They are kids who have *lost the belief that it is within their capacity to positively affect their own lives.* Having lost hope, they have learned to be helpless. They have little or no motivation or incentive to achieve and are not interested in learning new ways to cope with life's struggles. Their natural joy of learning seems to be gone and learning is thus dramatically delayed. They won't readily accept praise, gifts or kindness, and are unaffected by criticism. They seem apathetic, disinterested, and hopeless. Even the simplest solution to a problem seems outside the realm of their comprehension. This resembles depression, but is different. Depression is more pervasive but learned helplessness functions primarily within a system.

**Kids who have learned to be helpless
have lost the belief that it is within their
capacity to positively affect their own lives.**

Learned helplessness has likely been around forever but it wasn't until the last century that it started to be understood as anything different from depression or a circumstance where someone "quit on life." While many kids respond well to pressure and believe they can better their futures, our schools see numerous kids who don't. At home, a child struggling with learned helplessness is often found in his bedroom lying on his bed with ear buds on.

THE ORIGIN OF THE CONCEPT

To understand this term and this theory, we need to tie together several concepts from dogs, sheep, floors that shock, high expectations, stress, and "helping" our kids.

In 1941, in the early days in the field of behavioral psychology a group studying the problems of neurotic behavior sponsored a study. The findings of "Experimental Neurosis," by O. D. Anderson and Richard Parmenter, published by Cornell University, were fascinating, but the study received little attention.

In 1967, another study was published that became more well known in professional journals, yet received little attention by the general public. The findings resulted in a series of studies conducted by American psychologist Martin Seligman (who coined the term *learned helplessness*) and his colleagues at the University of Pennsylvania. By 1967, the word *neurotic* had lost its usefulness or appeal to many in the field of psychology. Therefore the stated purpose of Seligman's study was to understand *depression.*

Quite by accident, Seligman discovered that the conditioning of dogs led to outcomes that opposed the predictions of behavioral psychologists at the time. In these studies, dogs were used to test certain effects of classical conditioning. Ivan Pavlov and his dog experiments made classical conditioning (Pavlovian conditioning) famous. His dogs would salivate when they heard a tone that was sounded just prior to feeding. Soon the dogs would salivate at the tone, even before they were given their food.

Both of these studies found that a certain pattern of conditioning created responses of high anxiety or depression in the animals. Anderson and Parmenter's 1941 study concluded the anxiety of the dogs and sheep peaked when they could not figure out the link between the warning sound and the reinforcement. In short, the dogs were at times called upon to "solve" association problems—to distinguish between one stimulus and another. One stimulus would be reinforced with food and the other not reinforced. It didn't matter if the reinforcement was positive or negative. When the dogs and sheep couldn't figure this out, their behavior would shift markedly.

The study concluded the animals became considerably distressed and "showed a state of profound inhibition" when the problems facing them were beyond the animals' ability to achieve or decode. These dogs would eventually give up and start functioning in an avoidant, anxious, and distressed manner that was evident by measurements of their behavior, heart rate, breathing, and posture. These changes did not go away, even years later.

In Seligman's research, the behavior of three groups of dogs was evaluated. In the first group, dogs were strapped into harnesses for a period of time and then released. The dogs in the second group were placed in the same harnesses, but were subjected to electrical shocks that could be avoided by pressing a panel with their noses. The third group received the same shocks as those in group two, except they were not able to control the duration of the shock. For the dogs in the third group, the shocks seemed to be completely random and outside of their control. Group three dogs learned they had no influence over whether they were shocked or not.

In this study the concept of learned helplessness was discovered accidentally.

Seligman inadvertently discovered that dogs that had received unpredictable electric shocks failed to take action in subsequent situations—even those in which escape or avoidance was in fact possible. Surprising to most behavioralists at the time, this scenario resulted in the dogs simply lying down passively and whining. Even though they could have easily escaped the shocks, and the shocks were not too severe, the dogs didn't try because they didn't know when they were coming or to what they might be connected. But dogs that had not received the random shocks immediately took action in subsequent situations.

In both these experiments, the animals that believed they had no ability to affect or predict the shock or the reward behaved in ways that suggested they were troubled, fatigued, and hopeless. The animals' response was to quit everything. The 1941 study described "difficult differentiations" as the main contributor to the quit and anxiety observed. In other words, the animals couldn't predict what was coming next because they couldn't decode any connection with the stimulus and shock. They called this reaction *"experimental neurosis."* This reaction resulted in an estimated seven hundred percent increase in anxiety behaviors. In the 1967 experiment, the dogs that believed they had no control over what happened to them passively quit. Seligman is credited with being the first to use the phrase *"learned helplessness"* and it has been used and studied since this time.

The impact of learned helplessness has been demonstrated in a number of different animal species, but its features and characteristics can also be seen in humans. Learned helplessness is the condition in a human or animal that has learned to behave helplessly. In this condition, subjects fail to respond to their environment, even though there are opportunities for the subject to avoid a painful situation. As a result, they have almost no ability to adapt to changes in their life or environment.

[For those interested in these types of studies, classical conditioning involves pairing two stimuli together to get a response. It differs from operant conditioning, in which a behavior in a subject is strengthened or weakened by a reward or punishment. Both classical and operant conditioning can be administered in a way that creates learned helplessness.]

How Does This Relate to Kids?

Professionals who work with youth note that when some children adopt the view that they cannot understand or change a situation, they begin to truly believe there is nothing they can do to better their condition. These kids quickly become depressed, anxious, helpless, sad, or bored, and their learning slows to nearly a halt. Performance deteriorates as they become less likely to solve problems, even when the problems are identical to those solved before their helplessness set in. Essentially, they quit and lie down, not caring when the next "shock" is coming.

We started writing this book when a troubling observation

turned into a question, "Why are teenagers today acting in similar, predictable, and peculiar ways?" After years of working professionally with teens, we noticed a pattern of teens withdrawing to their rooms with seemingly unwarranted fatigue and hopelessness. This appeared to be more prevalent in adolescents than we had seen in previous decades. We then, like many others, noticed a sobering parallel.

Those earlier animal experiments (along with dozens of others not cited here) gave clues to what was going on in adults and children who experienced learned helplessness.

- When adults or children cannot predict the response to their behavior, or they are unable to decode what will bring punishment or reward, significant anxiety is created. This anxiety dramatically slows learning and they become indifferent to praise or criticism.

- When adults or children come to believe they have no real ability to control the outcome of their situations, they quit trying. Achievements in their lives are replaced with boredom, helplessness, anxiety, withdrawal, and depression. This dramatically slows learning.

Logic is no longer a factor when learned helplessness sets in. We see this with kids who were once social and resourceful but are now paralyzed by the simplest tasks. An example is a student who performs poorly on math tests and assignments, then studies hard and still fails a unit test. Over time he begins to believe that *nothing* he does will have any effect on his math performance. When later faced with any type of math-related task, he may experience a sense of helplessness. He won't even attempt to do math problems he may have completed successfully two years before. Learned helplessness has set in and a new problem, other than math, has been created.

This connection appears to be supported by the frequent number of teens, who in moments of unguarded honesty, say they feel they can never do anything "good enough."

IT'S NOT LAZINESS

From these kids' perspective, effort seems futile so they give up trying. But, it isn't out of laziness. This is important to remember. They procrastinate and only accomplish tasks that require little effort. They may meekly strive for unattainable goals, but they won't strive for any attainable goals. It is almost as if they are avoiding any positive completion of a task. They look depressed, and in this state, are often angry. They feel that they are too stupid to learn so, *why try?* Or they may wonder why everything for them is so difficult compared to their peers.

Learned helplessness creates three basic deficits in the child—cognitive, emotional, and motivational—all of which destroy the child's desire to learn. In the motivational deficit, learning stops when the necessary hope and predictability of life is missing. Too often it is said that the child is not trying, but research shows when these children have learned to be helpless, it is no longer an issue of effort. The learned helpless child believes he has no control over his world or the learning process, and it hurts too much to try.

There certainly was nothing lazy about the animals in the experiments and this is not an issue of laziness in kids. Those experimental dogs must have felt like they were locked in an emotional room with no door to the outside. With no escape in sight, there was no reason for them to try. Many teenagers find themselves in this same predicament and though it may look as if they don't care, more accurately, they have lost hope.

How This Occurs in Families

Something is happening in some families in our culture that is creating learned helplessness. We knew this was true from our own experience, and it can be powerfully validated by just a few Google searches on the topic. Hundreds, maybe thousands, of professionals and researchers have come to the same conclusions. We know it is true, but that doesn't mean we have totally figured out how it happens. Here are some theories.

In both of the experiments cited in this chapter the source of pain that the study animal responded to was electrical shock. The shock for the teenagers can be anything painful. Life produces discomfort on a regular basis: homework, rejection, chores, failure or scolding—basically anything. Pain or difficulty isn't the problem; nor is the quantity of pain and difficulty. The problem is when the subject feels helpless and hopeless to control or alter the pain that is present.

The Effect of Alcoholic Homes

Our first professional exposure to explicit learned helplessness was watching clients raised in alcoholic homes. We noticed right away that they *did not* believe they could influence or sway a good outcome out of even the most basic situations. They did believe they could medicate their pain, but not that they could avoid it or produce any type of victory out of a circumstance. With these individuals, it was clear their lives were missing the linear functioning needed for problem solving. While they needed to learn and believe they could piece solutions together, this eluded them.

An overly simplified explanation is that the positive or negative reinforcement they received in their alcoholic homes had nothing to do with their performance and was outside their realm of predictability. As kids, these people had no confidence at all that putting a series of good choices together would actually pay off for them. They didn't believe cleaning the kitchen, mowing the lawn, or doing homework would be consistently noticed or appreciated. As kids, they could have been yelled at for doing those things instead of being thanked. Receiving love, affection, or insults and rejection depended more on where the alcoholic parent was in his or her addictive remorse cycle than it depended on the child's performance or pleasantness. Likewise, these kids could break curfew, hit a sibling, or fail a unit in math. If this coincided with the alcoholic parent's guilt and contrition about excessive drinking, the child might have received praise and affection.

Too often favorable and unfavorable outcomes in the child's world were tied to a variable that had nothing to do with the child's conduct. This is far too complicated and dubious for any child to decode. The dynamic creates a depression and helplessness that sometimes lasts a lifetime. These kids, like the dogs and sheep, couldn't figure out what was coming next or how to decode the family system.

It is important to note here that even the rewards (food, praise, affection, presents, etc.), mean little to these kids because they don't know when or why a reward comes. The animals in the studies wouldn't even eat a treat, because they didn't know when the shock was coming. Many kids in alcoholic homes won't accept the love from a gift or embrace because they don't understand why it is coming right now or what might be coming next.

The main point here is: randomness is often the rule in

dysfunctional homes. Addictions, affairs, painful marriages, secrets, absence, media, and chaos can all contribute to an environment that is too irregular and unpredictable for a child to figure out and so feel secure.

It's All Around Us

It is interesting that this pervasive pattern doesn't just exist in troubled homes; we are now seeing evidence of learned helplessness in higher functioning homes and throughout society.

Let's look at the sources of pain in kids, the rewards they really want, and the systems they need to decode.

We believe kids really want (the reward):

- Inner peace
- Clarity of expectations
- To believe they are competent
- To know when they are done
- To believe that a task is achievable
- To believe good enough is good enough
- To learn tasks at a suitable age and developmental stage

We believe they don't want (the adverse stimuli or shock):

- Confusing stress
- Ambiguity in parents' moods and expectations
- To feel not capable
- Never feeling done

- Expectations that seem impossible or shifting
- To feel they are defective when they do anything short of excellent
- To be on guard or on call all the time

What we believe kids want to understand:

- Life isn't easy and won't feel that way
- When they're not on track
- That they are loved
- To know what is expected of them
- To know that if they do what is expected, more won't be added
- To predict somewhat accurately when they are or aren't in trouble
- To know there is help for them when they are stuck (but not too much help so they feel defective)

OVER-FUNCTIONING PARENTS

Hovering or over-functioning parents are often identified as major contributors to learned helplessness in kids. Over-functioning by one or both parents usually opens the door to a child under-functioning. These are the parents who are overly helpful and do too much for their kids.

In the home it can look like this: one of the parents wakes up an older child in the morning, makes his lunch, gathers all the essentials for the teenager's backpack while watching the clock to make sure he is on time. This behavior is undoubtedly a contributor to learned helplessness. Kids want to feel at peace and competent in their lives. While they are grateful for mom or dad's help, all this help severely threatens their sense that they can manage their lives on their own in a sufficient manner.

Hovering parents are certainly part of the problem, but there is much more to it than that. Stress is another contributor to learned helplessness.

THE VICIOUS CYCLE OF ACHIEVEMENT STRESS

Learned helplessness causes stress and anxiety—but stress and anxiety also causes learned helplessness. We feel stressed when we are ill prepared for something. The stress creates fear, and fear slows or stops learning so we can't get out in front of the challenge.

The stresses on today's children are too many to enumerate. At least half of them are unnecessary. For one, kids are hurried along in their growth. They are tested, ranked, pushed, and pressured—from admission tests to get into kindergarten all the way through to college-level advanced placement classes starting as early as the junior year of high school. Everything from sex education to algebra is taught earlier and earlier. Schools and parents, trying to cram their children (students) into the top five percent of society, compete in one-upmanship.

Some kids respond well to pressure and it brings out a wonderful side in them. But others don't handle pressure and stress well and it stifles their learning and their creativity. When these kids are confronted with tasks they are not ready for, they blame themselves for their deficiencies.

This is an important distinction. There is a difference between *knowing how to achieve something and being ready to achieve something.* One sixteen-year-old may be ready to drive a car in city traffic, whereas another sixteen-year-old may know how to drive, but not be ready to drive in city traffic. When a child knows he isn't ready to drive in traffic and life pressure tells him he should be ready, he feels defective. Some kids have the GPA and cognitive ability to handle college academics, but are not ready for college. When parents, teachers, adults, or peers tell a teenager he should be ready to do something and he isn't the teen may think: *There must be something wrong with me.*

Kids who don't rise to the challenge in pressure situations and who conclude they are defective because they are not ready for something when others say they should be are candidates for learned helplessness. The age at which children are ready for sleepovers, contact sports, being home alone for a couple days, college, babysitting, calculus, dirty jokes, or study abroad are all very different. Learned helplessness can result from pressure to enter into a world for which the child is not developmentally ready.

SOCIAL STRESS

Unbeknownst to many, it is stressful for kids to hang out with peers that are holding back their growth. Often teenagers will choose the short-term gain of immediate acceptance over the long term gain of growth. It is a subconscious decision to choose friends that will quickly and easily accept you rather than choosing a group of friends that have growth or accomplishment as a goal. For all kids, the quickest bond is with other kids that are expecting little of themselves. Shoplifting or stealing test answers can result in immediate recognition or approval from a group that is not growing.

Even when kids fight feverishly for the right to choose their own friends, it is very stressful for them when they choose

friends that are behind them on the *maturity* curve. The fear
of not being ready for adulthood, the fear of not being ready for
responsibilities, and the constant fear of getting caught creates a
chronic stress that can build semester by semester.

> *For those who will not allow you to move forward*
> *will eventually lead you backwards*
> *for nothing that stands behind*
> *will invite you to move ahead.*

Words Through Life,
- Bethanne Stafford

It is for this reason that parents need to intervene when kids
make poor friend choices. Too often parents are tentative or
reluctant to fight this battle. This is a battle worth fighting since
friends have a powerful impact on our kid's choices and growth.
"Show me your friends and I'll show you your future" is a saying
that is recited by professionals who work with youth. While
this is not always true, it is true enough to make us pause and
consider the effect problem friends can have on our kids.

Technology also adds significant social stress to kids. Junior-
high kids who may have no interest in texting fifty times a day
feel pressure to keep up with responding to text chains. They
feel pressure when they don't understand slang in a text. They
feel stress if they text too little or too much. Teasing texts,
flirting texts, texts that suddenly and unexplainably stop, texts
in the middle of the night, and texts that don't make sense are
all stressors for kids. When kids have no control over what is
said about them, good or bad, they feel helpless. They feel they
can't stop, because it is too stressful to not be part of the social
"conversation."

As recent as fifteen years ago, kids got a much-needed social breather when they were at home for a night or out on a family outing. There are no breathers now. Kids spend hundreds of hours monitoring Facebook, Twitter, and texts just to make sure they are aware of what is being said about them. There is stress around the social hierarchy that comes with what phone they have, what X-Box games are in their collection, and how many "friends" they have on Facebook.

Much of social networking for kids is outside their control and can make life feel scary and make children feel powerless. How can a kid control what is said about her or why she was left off a text chain? Social networking has made everything personal and so rapidly paced and kids feel the weight of it all.

THE MOVING CARROT

In many homes, especially conscientious homes, there is eagerness by the parents for the child to have ever-increasing achievements. Usually this is motivated by love, but this mimics the studies using dogs and shocks.

Here is how it looks: a teenager is given a limited list of expectations. She believes that this covers the scope of what is expected of her. In other words she believes she knows how to avoid "the shock in the floor." It might sound like, "All we expect is that you turn in all your assignments, study for your tests, and help out a little around the house." The girl uses this to build a rough perception of what is expected of her. The "reward" she is looking for is to feel like she is *done* with what is expected of her, (One of the stressors for adults and children is that they never feel done).

Then slowly, over the next several months, forty new expectations get added: clean the kitchen, lose five pounds, watch your little brother, start violin lessons, go to temple, unload the groceries, clean your room, etc. Over months and even years this girl stops believing that she is ever going to be *done*. Being done is the reward she is subconsciously looking for.

There is nothing wrong with holding to many expectations for a child. However, there is something terribly wrong with a home life where a child lives perpetually on guard. Some teenagers may have four or five corrective comments made to him just during the course of making a snack. You can see the parallels to the animal studies, assuming that peace or "being done" is the reward the child is looking for, and nagging or reminders are the shock. The teen cannot figure out what to do to stop the corrections.

Negative reinforcement is a form of operant conditioning that has been tied to learned helplessness. This simply means that something unwanted (adverse) stops temporarily when the dog does the desired behavior. It seems like this should work, but it only works for a while, then the dog quits and makes no effort to relieve the pain even though it knows how to.

We have often observed families where criticizing and nagging stop temporarily when a child does the right thing. The dictionary describes nagging as: "continually complaining or faultfinding." Faultfinding can be very easy to do when we have a child who is falling short on so many fronts. A truly loving parent may easily convince himself that he is not faultfinding but just pointing out the numerous shortcomings in his thirteen-year-old's behavior. This is another reminder: *parent quietly.*

THE HOLE IS TOO DEEP

Imagine a boy taking part in an outdoor endurance event. His legs are well muscled and he can step up to fifteen inches.

If he were put into a fourteen-inch-deep hole in the ground, stepping out would be easily accomplished even with his hands tied. In a hole four inches deeper, escaping would be very problematic.

Whether it is missed ACT tests, six English assignments due, no money, a messy room, lost friends, lost status or a lost passion for life—kids with learned helplessness often have dug a hole too deep to get out of in one step. It drives parents crazy when a child they love more than life itself, who is wonderful and precious, repeatedly messes up eight things a day and does virtually nothing right. How do you help a child when too much help partially created the mess in the first place? Parents feel damned if they do and damned if they don't.

This is a legitimate and real problem and we want you to know that you are not alone. Thousands of parents feel the same way.

It's All About Perceptions

Learned helplessness is all about perceptions. We are all driven by our perceptions of expectations, and also by hope, opportunity, learning, and even hopelessness. We repeatedly take in information and pass it through our belief systems and come out with perceptions. These can be accurate or inaccurate but they drive our lives.

When we meet someone and she tells us about an event in her life, she is telling us the information she took in, the belief she has about that information, and her experience or perceptions of the event. This usually happens beyond her awareness. She thinks she is just telling us what happened.

We all see events and then pass that data through a belief system, even before we actually know what happened. In the case of learned helplessness the belief is, "I don't believe I can figure out how this system works," or, "I don't believe I can affect the outcome of the challenge before me." Once that belief sets in, it affects how we experience every challenge. Your child didn't suddenly become helpless—he just suddenly believed he was. His perception became his reality.

People stuck in dead-end jobs, those fighting a second or third bout with cancer, heavy smokers who have tried numerous times to quit, alcoholics, some with obesity, or people stuck in abusive relationships are all likely candidates for learned helplessness. This can happen to anyone who believes life will never get any better. Anyone who has been shocked too many times and can't decode how life works can surrender to this belief.

HELP FOR THE HELPLESS

- Have compassion on these kids—they aren't lazy or bad.

- If you over-function as a parent, gradually cut back on your help, reminders, and doing things for your child. Part of their under-functioning is you over-functioning.

- Hold your child accountable to minimal reasonable expectations. (It won't help to give too much grace).

- Clearly and briefly tell him that he has or hasn't met your expectations, but that you are neither thrilled nor angry. Use minimal encouragement or criticism—just the facts.

- Offer to work with him in the beginning. *Do not* do anything *for* him. Working *with* him is immensely healing. If he quits, you quit. Often a tutor with a contagious love of learning can help with this role.

- Focus on The Two Things discussed in Chapter Twelve.

- When it is true, tell him he is doing fine. Tell him to relax. Tell him he is "done" for the day. Say it as often as you can when it is true.

- Let the little stuff go while holding the line on what you have agreed to. If your child is developmentally behind, focusing on too many things will cause another setback.

- Reinforce with your child that he is on his own timetable and you aren't worried about racing other kids to the finish line.

- As a favor to your children, occasionally disconnect them from technology so they can find some peace. Don't let them take their smartphones to bed, to grandma's, on a walk, out on the boat, etc. It may be more convincing if you are willing to shut yours off in these situations, too.

- Repeatedly affirm that you aren't worried about how he'll turn out in the end. He might not go from high school to college, but if he does go to college he will be ready for the challenge. (If your child is using drugs, depressed, hanging with a dangerous crowd, cutting, etc., then certainly tell him you are worried or concerned).

- Do not allow excessive isolating.

- Let good enough be good enough. A child with learned helplessness may be a great kid, but he is never going to be an overachiever or exceptional in any measurable way until his beliefs change. That is fine. Just enjoy him.

- Allow him to struggle and experience the cost of underachieving. Take away his car or X-Box privileges. Remember: the problem isn't that he can't handle life; the problem is he believes he can't decode life. (This is why many kids will drop the helplessness and do well at deer hunting or whitewater kayaking, or golf, or boarding. Those are arenas where they believe they have control and they know the rules). Make your rules at home believable.

- Do not nag your child. Their beliefs are made up of words and it is words and anger that perpetuate the problem. Be creative and think of another solution that doesn't involve repeating a request or a criticism.

- Changing the rules or expectations based on the child's mood or level of being overwhelmed adds to the problem. Remember you are trying to create a system that is unambiguous and believable. Who would respect a system that changed every time someone's mood changed?

The GIST of It

- When children lose the belief that they have the capacity to positively affect their own lives, they lose hope and learn to be helpless.

- Unpredictable households can be a contributor to learned helplessness.

- Learned helplessness results in the child's inability to adapt to changes in his life or environment.

- Kids can recover when they learn they can control the outcomes in their lives and experience success.

Chapter Twenty-Two:
The Impact of Stress

Benjamin's Story

On the outside, Benjamin looked like a sixteen-year-old young man who functioned at a high level. He was popular at school, played varsity sports, achieved academically, and participated in a variety of extracurricular activities. To all appearances, he was a nice, well-rounded young man. Yet, Benjamin was in turmoil with a combination of anxiety, fear, and anger. He lived an emotional roller coaster on the inside while portraying a life of achievement and success.

Benjamin was an expert secret keeper. His father was present in the home but fighting his own demons. His mother suffered severe depression. Their marriage was falling apart, and the family's financial situation was treading water.

He knew all the details of his parents' reality. His entire identity was wrapped up in not letting the world know his home life was the opposite of what the world thought it was. He struggled to fall asleep, felt like his mind was always going a million miles an hour, and lived with an intense and constant fear that his friends might someday find out about what he had to deal with at home. He was anxious and frequently experienced panic attacks. He worked very hard at keeping everything looking good—anything to prevent the real truth from being known by the world.

Benjamin was experiencing stress.

Megan's Story

On the other end of the spectrum, Megan was a girl who might be described as a "wallflower." She was average at almost everything she tried: grades, number of friends, sports and music abilities, and life in general. Nothing was wrong with Megan. She was fine just the way she was— she was just average.

But, influenced by the culture around her, Megan compared herself to every above-average girl in her class and always felt like a failure. She told herself, *You'll never be really good at anything.* She worried about not having a boyfriend, not being in the popular group at school, not being smart enough to go to college, and not having a nice complexion.

Every day she experienced life defeated, hopeless, and stressed, except for the days she made herself mindlessly busy. On those days she experienced mostly nothing. Most days she just wanted to give up. She told herself that her life would always be meaningless and futile. Many times she thought of running away and starting new somewhere else where she might be able to be above average. She even thought about ending her life, yet wasn't sure that she would succeed at that.

Megan was experiencing stress.

Parents need to know how much stress can influence their child. To help understand this, we'd like to address what happens in the child's body when he or she becomes stressed. This stress leads to predictable and sometimes bizarre behaviors. The hope is that parents will not only better recognize stress in their child, but respond in ways that foster their child's ability to deal with stress now and in the future.

THE STRESS REACTION

When a child experiences an emergency, there is a release of stress hormones in his body. In turn these hormones mobilize what is physiologically needed to deal with the situation. A frightening movie scene, being chased by a vicious dog, falling, or any traumatic experience can trigger this stress hormone release. This normal process helps kids protect themselves from danger or injury. Adults also have a similar release of stress hormones to deal with emergencies in their lives, although adult emergencies tend to be different.

There are two major systems that produce stress hormones. The sympathetic adrenomedullary system (SAM) produces adrenaline from the adrenal glands that lie just above the kidneys. Adrenaline quickly gives us the "fight or flight" response that we need to protect ourselves when we are in danger. Our bodies can produce adrenaline in a split second. Adrenaline increases the heart rate and diverts blood away from the gut and skin (which are nonessential in an emergency) allowing more blood to be available to muscles and the brain. Our blood sugar increases due to the effect of adrenaline on the liver, and this energy source allows us to react to stress situations. Most people know when this "right now" hormone enters their bloodstream.

The second stress hormone is cortisol and it is released through the hypothalamic-pituitary-adrenal system (HPA). Cortisol, which is also produced in the adrenal glands, takes longer to produce in our bodies (about twenty-five minutes), but it has a longer lasting effect. Cortisol reacts with receptors inside of the cell, regulating gene transcription and modulating metabolism at the cellular level. Eventually, the body experiences physiological and behavioral changes.

How Children Are Affected

It is just beginning to be understood how stress affects the brains of young children. We know that newborns have low levels of cortisol in their bloodstreams and those levels increase the first six months of life. Around three months of age, the infant's cortisol patterns start to look more like adult patterns, including a circadian peak of cortisol release in the early morning. We know that babies experience an increase in levels of cortisol during medical examinations, blood draws, and other traumatic events. Repeated exposures to stress will induce chronic increases of cortisol, leading to an increase in fear behaviors, increased caution, and symptoms similar to PTSD.

Stress also can have a detrimental effect on brain function, including cognition and memory. The presence of higher cortisol levels in infants and young children is associated with smaller electrical changes in the brain during memory formation. New memory formation is impaired. Nursery school or daycare-age children who have high cortisol levels have a more difficult time maintaining attention. Attention span is an important factor in a child's ability to self-regulate. These children have more trouble maintaining self-control because of their higher cortisol levels.

In summary, cortisol from stress plays an important role in memory formation, attention span, and self-regulating behaviors in children. One must wonder if there is a connection between increased stress in children and the epidemic of ADD/ADHD, relative lack of self-regulating behaviors, and academic underachievement.

Children who experience chronic and high levels of stress appear to have even more significant consequences. As mentioned before, stress increases cortisol levels in our bodies. Once the stress is relieved, cortisol levels return to normal. But, in children who have high and longstanding stress, cortisol levels remain high, even after the stress has been appropriately dealt with. Children with chronically elevated levels of cortisol show problems with their motor development, physical health, social skills, and mental function. They tend to function in a state of fear and their coping mechanisms become habitual.

Stress is encountered in four different stages of early childhood. In the first stage, alarm sets in. The child experiences a surge of adrenaline and feels afraid and agitated. In the second stage, the child appraises the situation and tries to find meaning in what has happened. Stage three is when the child tries to figure out how to cope with the new reality. He may develop several possible ways to deal with the stress he is experiencing or he may not figure out any way that helps him through his difficulty. Stage four is when the child executes one or more of the coping strategies. A child who has a low natural ability to deal with adversity may experience alarm in certain situations quicker than average and may experience stress with milder and more varied stress opportunities. He will often exist in a chronic state of stress and disruption.

SIGNS AND SYMPTOMS OF STRESS

Kids can be quite good at disguising their stress but the signs and symptoms are many. Parents often don't want to think that their child is stressed-out; they would rather have a medical reason for their child's symptoms. Parents and doctors may go down roads of evaluation that ultimately delay discovering what is really going on with the child.

Signs and symptoms of stress can be categorized into four areas: physical, behavioral, emotional, and cognitive. Although the following lists are not exhaustive, it's clear that much of what brings patients to the office of a psychologist or pediatrician can be attributed to stress in the child's life or family. A thorough medical and psychological evaluation may be needed to determine what is causing the child's symptoms.

Much of what brings children to the office of a psychologist or a pediatrician can be attributed to stress in the child's life or family.

Physical symptoms of severe stress might include any one or several of the following: chronic abdominal pain, headaches, diarrhea, constipation, dizziness, nausea and vomiting, chest pain, heart palpitations, frequent colds, and body or muscle aches. Behavioral symptoms of stress include increased or decreased appetite, sleeping a lot or not enough, isolating, neglecting responsibilities, abusing drugs or alcohol, annoying behavior, and nervous habits like nail biting and picking.

Emotional symptoms include moodiness, depression, agitation, being short-tempered, and feeling overwhelmed. Some children experience cognitive symptoms of stress such as poor memory, concentration difficulties, excessive worrying, negativity, and inappropriate judgment. It is not uncommon to find kids going through divorce in their families who struggle with academics and focus.

The Three Kinds of Stress

Not all stress is bad. In fact, stress can be an important part of a child learning resilience or responding appropriately to a threat. Many experts believe there are three kinds of stress: positive stress, tolerable stress, and toxic stress. As clinicians, we tend to see the children in the second or third categories.

Positive stress usually comes from situational and short duration adversity. This might include a spelling test or a first sleepover. This stress may cause minor hormonal fluctuations and physiological adjustment. With appropriate support of the adults in their lives, children learn the skill of overcoming stress and adversity.

Tolerable stress results from more significant events, which might include losing a close relative, moving away from long-term friends, experiencing a house fire, or having a significant illness. Tolerable stress causes a more significant physiological response in stress hormone levels, but with time and appropriate adult support, the child eventually recovers and returns to their normal physiologic state.

Toxic stress is a different animal. It activates both arms of the body's stress response to very high levels and for long periods of time. Examples of toxic stress include chronic neglect, emotional or physical abuse, exposure to family violence, homelessness, and severe economic hardship, to name a few. Without the support of positive adults who are not contributing to the child's stress, these kids grow up with stress-induced diseases like depression, substance abuse, and heart disease. The more a child is exposed to toxic stress, the more likely he or she is to develop later problems. The good news is that the effects of toxic stress can be prevented and reversed in children with early adult intervention and changes to the child's environment and caretakers.

HELPING CHILDREN THROUGH STRESSFUL SITUATIONS

Some kids are unable to cope with life's challenges and stresses in preschool, middle school, and beyond. Too many children are growing up on medication to help them stay calm, react less, pay attention, be more pleasant, be happy, and not self-destruct. Some children have a way of thinking that is truly distorted from reality. Most of these children have experienced events that have changed them, but were never guided through these events to resolution, closure, or a healthy perspective.

THERE ARE WAYS TO PARENT THAT WILL RADICALLY REDUCE STRESS IN OUR CHILDREN'S LIVES.

Think back to a major event in your life and consider how poorly or how effectively the adults in your life handled it. How would you have turned out if your parents, coaches, or other adults had handled major events in your childhood differently?

We see many example of this, good and bad, with our patients. Thankfully, many divorces today are handled in ways that are respectful to kids and minimize the stress they experience. However, divorce is sometimes handled in ways that leave scars in the children and families involved. Parents who have separated or divorced are experiencing pain themselves and can unintentionally manipulate their children to fit their reality. They may blame the divorce on their former spouse with little consideration of how this negativity may affect their children.

The divorce event can take on a life of its own which includes lies, defamation, revenge, hate, spite, and hostage taking. The children may not be helped to understand the separation in age-appropriate ways. The resulting experience for the child is stressful, confusing, and negative. It is no wonder so many adults recall such negative and hurtful memories about their parents' messy divorce decades earlier. (When handled in a kind and thoughtful way, kids can recover nicely from a divorce).

Another example of a stress dynamic is the preteen girl who's cute but average looking, doesn't fit into skinny jeans, isn't in the popular group at school, and has little athletic ability. This compilation of factors could be considered an "event." Janis Ian's song "At Seventeen" is poetry set to music describing this scenario. How should parents handle this situation so the daughter has a chance of growing, maturing, and thriving through this time in her life?

Many parents respond by giving their daughter the false message that she is just as pretty as the other girls. But the daughter's idea of pretty or beautiful is based on Photoshopped faces on the cover of teen magazines. Her feeling of unattractiveness at school is the reality she lives in every day. No matter what her parents say to her about her being beautiful or pretty, it won't convince her.

Do You Respond or Overreact?

Some parents overreact to their child's stress and some underreact. The goal is to figure out how to appropriately respond. The appropriate parental response in handling events in their child's life uses positive stress, and provides healthy coping skills, learning, and cross application. Remember, the goal is not to have your child be stress-free. This is not to say that the parents' way of handling stressful events in their child's life affects the outcome one hundred percent, but it is one of the most important factors.

Let's start with an event that induces stress in a child's life. It matters not what it is, just that it elicits a stress response in the child. The child's stress hormones then kick in. Cortisol and adrenaline run through her bloodstream. The parents have a choice on how to respond: overreaction or guidance. Each parental response has its own implications for the child and the family.

The over reactive parent fuels the stress hormones in the child by elevating the arousal state of their child and themselves. Due to their response, they create an environment where it's difficult for anyone to think logically. Everything becomes emotional for the child *and* the parent. This stress cycle builds and builds into a vicious dynamic for everyone involved.

The guiding parent sees stress in his child and responds to it in a way that helps define how much or how little stress the event really deserves. The primary form of guidance should be guiding the child *about* the problem, not necessarily guiding him through the problem.

Helping Kids View the Problem

A child who completely loses her temper on finding a rip in her pants needs help adjusting her reaction. This stress might be ranked a two out of ten when she is reacting as if it were an eight out of ten. Comments like *This is really not a big deal; I can fix them,* or, *We have time to go home and get a different pair of pants,* should be utilized rather than helping her process the situation as if it were an eight in importance.

The parent's goal is to reassure the child that this event is a little speed bump in life, not a sinkhole. Because your child sees an event as a disaster does not mean that it *is* a disaster and should not be responded to as such. Do not let your child define the seriousness or importance of a stressful event. Parents need to do the defining.

Stress is a potential learning opportunity for the child. Lots of things affect the parents' ability to teach and guide: exhaustion, impatience, marital discord, work, family illness, etc. Yet the parents' discipline of teaching and guiding their children is a critical way they eventually learn about life. As they say in Africa, "all young male elephants need a bull elephant."

Most importantly, remember many of the behaviors we see in our children are simply a manifestation of stress. Kids are bombarded with triggers that elicit a stress response: family turmoil, news reports, peer pressure, temptations, being overloaded, and a lack of margin, to name a few.

Your response to stress is pivotal in helping your child learn to handle stress more positively. Unfortunately, many parents react to a child's stress in ways that increase the stress. Parents need to be a calm and stable influence for their children, calling out their child's competence. If not, your child may never learn to put stressful events and dynamics into the proper perspective.

The GIST of It

- Stress causes predictable physiologic changes in children that can lead to complaints and behaviors that mimic a variety of diseases and maladies. Stress should be considered when medical causes have been eliminated.

- Kids who live in states of chronic stress can have permanent changes that may be difficult to normalize.

- Not all stress is bad. It can be helpful in teaching kids resilience and how to deal with adversity in their lives.

- A parent's overreaction to his child's stress makes the experienced stress worse. This makes it less likely the child will learn how to deal with stress in positive ways.

Final Words

We've presented our thoughts on parenting and believe the principles presented here offer a better way to parent than what is usually practiced. Remember, for you to "grow up" your children, *you* need to make the most changes. Consider how your parenting behavior affects your child before jumping to the conclusion that it is solely your child's problem. Parenting can be the most difficult and tasking endeavor of your life. There is nothing in this book or any other that can assure a parent of an easy road. In truth, some kids are really difficult. Some kids are easy, but some kids will require patience, focus, talent, and foresight – and this will still be a long, sometimes tiring journey. This is a book about efficiency and the likelihood of outcomes. We believe these principles are a parent's best chance at making parenting fun, exciting, and rewarding. That is all.

Looking at parenting differently will determine the amount of change that happens. We think you will be happier for it and live more peacefully.

The biggest benefit will be kids who grow up much more ready for life. The greatest fear of many parents centers around watching their kids reach adult age with no clue of how to manage their lives, themselves, or their relationships. That can be very painful for parents ... and for their young adults.

It doesn't matter what your child has been diagnosed with. What matters is that you start to understand what you need to do, or not do, to help him or her be ready for the adult world. Whether your child has been labeled difficult, high-spirited, stubborn, or feisty, you can adjust your parenting to fit the child.

Think about it this way: if your child has a degree of difficulty of eighty-five on a scale of one hundred, and your parenting ability is average (a fifty), you are going to have difficulty unless you learn ways of parenting that child at an eighty-five. Likewise, if you have a child who is super easy with a degree of difficulty of ten, you could be a below average parent and the child would turn out just fine.

Joy in the Journey

Simplifying life will be an integral part of your success as a parent. Simplifying will create positive memories and build relationships that are based on wanting to be together as a family unit. This does not necessarily mean family time with the entire family. Some kids respond much better to one-on-one time with a parent. Also, this doesn't mean your family can't have a hundred things going. It is possible to simplify without cutting back. Simplifying means less urgency, less intensity, less shame, and less anger. Whatever issue your family is facing, it will likely go better with a simple solution.

We also want all parents to have fun. When we look at things differently, creativity and spontaneity can become part of the norm again. Instead of experiencing each day frantic, discouraged, or disillusioned, we can enjoy the ride as we watch our kids grow up. Parenting was meant to be a wonderful adventure, not an exhausting plod. We've met too many parents who can't wait for their kids to leave the house. We say, take back the joy of the journey!

We strongly encourage you to develop and grow in your other relationships, too. This is such an important thing for your children to see. In the end, what parents pass on to their children will affect their children's generation as well as the generations beyond. Family dysfunction breeds more dysfunction. But all of us have the ability to learn to see things differently. Whether you are a single parent or a couple and whether your children are biological or adopted, challenged or gifted in any way, there is good news included in the pages of this book. Parents who were not parented very well have the ability to change the trajectory of their families now and in the future – and to do this with more peace and less effort.

-Notes